Development Planning at the Grassroots

About the Author

Dr. K.V.Sundaram, Geographer and Planner, started his career as a lecturer at Alagappah University and received his D.Litt degree from University of Mysore in 1977. He was awarded the prestigious Senior Nuffield Fellowship from UK (1978-79) for his post-doctoral work in the Centre for South-Asian Studies from Cambridge University.

His technical expertise covers Urban & Regional Planning, Economic and Human Resource Development. He worked with FAO, ESCAP, ICIMOD, CIRDAP, UNCRD and UNICEF in many Asian and African countries and with the Indian Planning Commission. He was also the resource person to World Bank, AIT (Bangkok), Karnataka Planning Board and India's 10th Plan. He has published 23 books and 220 research papers and was recently honoured by his friends and colleagues by a book called *Development Concerns in 21st Century.*

During his career he received a *Life Time Achievement Award by Centenarian Trust (Chennai)* and *Bhoogal Ratna Award by NAGI*. He was also felicitated at *Banaras Hindu University, Centre for Earth Sciences (Thiruvananthapuram),* and *University of Allahabad* and by the *Mayor of Philippines (1973).*

As the Founder Chairman of Bhoovigyan Vikas Foundation, he worked towards developing Earth Care Policies in Third World Countries. At the age of 83 he still dreams of establishing a National Care Policy Institute.

Development Planning at the Grassroots

K.V. SUNDARAM

CONCEPT PUBLISHING COMPANY PVT. LTD.,
NEW DELHI-110059

ISBN-13 : 978-81-8069-868-2

First Published 2012

Published and Printed by

Concept Publishing Company Pvt. Ltd.
A/15-16, Commercial Block, Mohan Garden
New Delhi-110059 (India)
T: 25351460, 25351794, *F*: 091-11-25357109
E: publishing@conceptpub.com, W: www.conceptpub.com
Editorial Office: H-13, Bali Nagar, New Delhi-110 015, India.

Cataloging in Publication Data--*Courtesy:* D.K. Agencies (P) Ltd. <docinfo@dkagencies.com>

Sundaram, K. V.
Development planning at the grassroots / K.V. Sundaram.
p. cm.
Includes bibliographical references and index.
ISBN 9788180698682

1. Regional planning—India. 2. Sustainable development—India. 3. Decentralization in government—India. I. Title.

DDC 352.2830954 23

The book is dedicated to

My Daughter

Late Mrs. Geeta Raghavan

M. Subramanian, IAS (Retd.)
Former Agriculture Secretary
Government of India.

347, Sector A, Pocket C
Vasant Kunj
New Delhi-110070.
July 16, 2011

Foreword

My friend Dr. K.V. Sundaram is unique in his multiple accomplishments. He is a leading Indian geographer of international repute. As founder chairman of the Bhoovigyan Vikas Foundation he has been a pioneer in the global and national campaign for saving Mother Earth and her natural resources with sustainable development. He is also a pioneer in the field of Decentralized Multi-level Local Area Planning. A distinguished academic, he demonstrated a remarkable ability to put his ideas into practice. For more than a decade, he was heading the concerned division in the Planning Commission and helped central ministries and state governments in the process of decentralized planning at regional and district levels.

The "blossoms" included in this book reflect the scenario of his vast knowledge and rich experience. There are seven chapters addressing the issues of Land Use Policy and Sustainable Development. Eight more chapters deal with Multi-level Local Area Planning. The remaining three chapters deal with the role of Information Technology. This is indeed a useful guidebook for academicians and government functionaries concerned with land use (with sustainable development) and decentralized planning (at regional and district levels). To the reader who will surely be fascinated by the clarity and down-to-earth approach of Dr. Sundaram, I may point out that these blossoms are only the latest of Dr. Sundaram's valuable published contributions. The reader should refer to Dr. Sundaram's earlier publications to get a more comprehensive picture of the subjects he has dealt with in this book.

I consider writing this Foreword a special honour for more than one reason. As Union Agriculture Secretary, I authored the National Land Use Policy Statement of 1986 (with the encouragement of Dr. Manmohan Singh, the present Prime Minister). Secondly, I had the opportunity of ushering in a New Industrial Locations Policy in Maharashtra which stipulated that industrial estates and new industries were to be located only in growth centres identified by the process of Area Planning for each region of the state. Thirdly, I could see and admire Dr. Sundaram's ability to translate his ideas on planning into action plans during my tenure with the Rural Development Ministry. Lastly, I recall the interdepartmental conflicts on matters relating to Land Use Policy to which I was witness as Union Agriculture Secretary. Everyone was paying lip service to the concept of sustainable development, but agencies responsible for speedy economic growth were always unhappy with our concerns or objections that related to appropriate land use. Perhaps the situation is no different today, looking at Dr. Jairam Ramesh's experience. A resolution of these conflicts can be done on a more scientific basis, if we listen to the voice of experts like Dr. Sundaram.

May God bless Dr. K.V. Sundaram and Mrs. Girija Sundaram (the pillar behind his success) with a long and prosperous life so that we can continue to benefit from his abundant knowledge and experience.

M. Subramanian

Preface

'Some Blossoms in the Wood' is a compilation of my eighteen Keynote and Presidential Addresses, delivered in various forums, during the last decade of my professional career, as Chairman, Earth Care Foundation. By and large, they cover the themes relating to Regional/ Area/Local Level Development and Decentralized Planning.

As a practitioner of Development Planning, who had the opportunity to work in national and international organizations, I have sought to reflect in this publication my personal experiences at the grassroots as well as policy level. In particular, in these lectures, the search for appropriate technologies and adaptive practices for achieving human development have been emphasised. I am grateful to my beloved wife, Mrs. Girija Sundaram, who undertook the painstaking task of locating these lectures from amidst a heap of papers in the house, arranging them, and in editing the book with necessary corrections.

The18 selected addresses included in this book have been arranged under the following heads;

1. Local Level Planning
2. Regional/Area Developments
3. Land Use Policy
4. Information Technology
5. Sustainable Development
6. Decentralized Planning

In conclusion, I acknowledge the intangible, but real inspiration and strength received through my faith in god's will, which has underlain my perseverance to the end.

Contents

IV
Information Technology

V
Sustainable Development

VI
Decentralised Planning

I
Local Level Planning

1

Role of Youth in Decentralised Planning and Rural Renaissance

Introduction

The focus of our discussion in this session is: How to institutionalise and energise the participation of youth at local levels in managing the development of their own communities.

Youth are undoubtedly our Social capital—the greatest human asset. Their active and energetic role in rural development needs to be harnessed and institutionalised for genuinely nurturing participatory planning, decision-making, and plan implementation by rural communities. Our experience with decentralised planning shows that people's active participation at the local level has not significantly advanced beyond their participation in periodical elections.

Decentralised Planning, as Self-reliant Development

Decentralised Planning with youth participation has remained for long only at the stage of good intentions. It is time that it now emerges as a potent propelling force and key to the transformation of India's villages. This calls for a new approach. Recognising the disciplinary limitations of public administration in promoting people-centred

---

* Key Note Address delivered in the Rajiv Gandhi National Institute of Youth Development, Sripeumpudur, Tamil Nadu-Published in the Journal, Endeavour, Vol. 1, Vol. 2, July-Dec 2007.

development and changes in power structure advocated by the radicals in our highly stratified social structure, the task of inducting the youth in the process of local level development planning has to be aggressively pursued as a movement in Rural Renaissance. Decentralised Planning in this context acquires a new meaning of self-reliant development, not only as a means but also as an end towards equitable social development. In the present era of globalisation and liberalisation with its emerging external constraints, it is becoming increasingly clear, that our rural areas will have to rely more on participation of individuals and local communities in solving their basic developmental problems. Some success stories in the country have shown that a significant development in this direction can be engineered through village youth, assisted by some catalytic agents from outside.

Motivations Needed for Youth for Operationalising Decentralised Planning

In the decentralised planning context, the youth have to be strongly motivated:

(i) In organising themselves under local leadership;
(ii) In identifying local developmental needs and socially relevant programmes and effectively operationalising them;
(iii) In formulating development plans for each village to meet the local needs, and mobilising local resources to supplement the resources coming from development agencies;
(iv) In organising self-help groups and community-based organisations, for initiating action plans, taking collective decisions to implement them, actively supporting the Panchayati Raj Institutions in bargaining and liaising with relevant Government agencies to obtain resources and effectively utilising them for development purposes.

Youth as the First Real Resource for Planning

All these tasks imply that the youth have to be trained and motivated in the first instance. Thus trained youth i.e. manpower--with human skill and effort—constitute our "first Real Resource" for planning. Along with manpower, we must also have a second set of "Real Resources", such as the various physical means of production. These are first and foremost the natural endowments, which provide the raw materials for production planning, coupled with an existing set of equipment or infrastructure including technology, needed to convert the primary resources into secondary goods. Technical processes fundamentally need the Real Resources for production. Without them, monetary resources are of no avail—a ten-dollar currency cannot turn a screw[1]. Lack of real resource considerations in planning is leading to the absence of 'social relevance' in our planning and this can be, by and large, corrected with the induction of youth into decentralised planning. Through the efforts of local youth trained as catalysts/social animators, the local community can be 'conscientized" and motivated to set up 'poly-centric' planning and implementation groups or organizations, who can relentlessly work for the welfare of their communities in various aspects of development. Thus, setting up people's own organisations, serves as the most effective weapon in the hands of local communities. In this manner, a participatory development process gets institutionalised, through which the local community becomes conscious enough, to assert its rights and begins to link up with government's delivery system. This hypothesis is quite contrary to the traditional view of "decentralisation", which is usually perceived in terms of "top-down transfer" of authority within a government framework[2].

Decentralised Planning as a 'Bottom up' Exercise

In terms of spatial levels, one may visualise Decentralised Planning as a multi-level exercise in five levels: the neighbourhood, the village, a cluster of 15 to 20 villages constituting a relatively homogenous community, the Development block and the District. Since any programme of development conceived from above should be responsive to the needs of the people, who are its beneficiaries, the felt needs as well as the initiatives for development should emerge from a group of people, who can articulate the people's needs and also throw some light on how these needs can be met—e.g. through self-help or outside help e.g. Governments, Banks, Technology groups etc. But even for forming such groups, interacting with them and to analyse and draw inferences about their priority needs, intelligent local youth are required, who can inspire confidence among the people and arrive at consensus on the priority needs, as well as methods of fulfilling these needs.

Planning at the village level should be performed through a *Village Planning Forum,* constituted by the Gram Sabha, by selecting some educated people or leaders in the village, assisted by local youth working as Social animators[3]. These animators should be drawn from the local community itself, who can work with farmers and other workers and can make things happen for the community.

The village level plan will have two major components:

(i) Planning for sectoral development programmes initiated by governments (like health care services, agricultural production, development of physical and social infrastructure and community development) . But such programmes should be sparked off through social animators, who should assist in their implementation, by setting up active local organisations, mostly community based, with strong participatory characteristics.

(ii) In addition, some Programmes should also be initiated by *locally self-managed groups*, in which local leaders will be playing a catalytic role, assisted by village youth. Such programmes are generally characterised by some efforts to mobilise the community's own resources, in order to become more self-reliant.

Village youth, acting as '*Social animators*' or '*Barefoot planners at the local level*', can play a crucial role and assist the village panchayat in preparing the village development plan based on the principles of "*Development from Within*"[4]. Such a plan will be a practical programme of action, responsive to the felt needs of the village population. It would aim at achieving the following six-fold goals[5] *viz.,*

1. Identification of resource potentials.
2. Identification of felt needs of the community.

3. A rational way of deciding priorities and programmes.
4. Some essential programmes to benefit the weaker sections of the community.
5. Identifying the beneficiaries of government-aided anti-poverty and employment programmes.
6. Conserving and managing the soil, water, vegetation and common property resources of the village.

Experience with micro-level planning in some massive rural development programmes, launched by Governments in India, Bangladesh and other countries of South Asia, while succeeding in setting up elaborate delivery mechanisms have, in most cases, failed to establish truly participatory grassroots organisations. On the other hand, the second category of local planning, tried through non-government initiatives and experiments seem to have been more successful. Some of them have become success stories and have complemented government's own efforts for decentralised rural development.

Success Stories

The Kundrakudi model of rural development in Tamil Nadu, (late 70's and early 80's), where some external and internal organisational factors determined its success, provides some clues about its positive impact on concepts of development and self-governance. This author, in his evaluation of the Kundrakudi experiment, conducted for the Planning Commission[6], identified the three vital elements of rural organisation building—which he called as "*Technocratic–Academic and Democratic mix (TAD MIX)*"[6a], which spelt its success. If such an association of dedicated technocrats, academics and community organisations, led by the local village panchayat, can come together and address the common issues of rural development, more authentic decentralised rural development can ensue.

Kerala's '*People's Campaign*', is a success story in the building up of Grassroot Planners. This has shown that such local level planners need to be nurtured and strengthened through a massive capability-building programme. Here, the selected youth within the community were given certain exposure to understand the social organisation of the village, provide leadership as well as promote leadership qualities within the community. They succeeded in building up Neighbourhood groups, User's Groups/Associations, Women's Groups and Self-help groups, to promote mutual dependence among the families, for economic activity and security[7].

In another success story in *Community Action Planning* in Tamil Nadu[8], a collaborative project initiated in 1999 by a group of researchers from India and Canada through a process of Community Action Planning addressed the restoration of the degraded environments in five villages of the Thevaram Basin. The project team, acting as catalysts and resource persons to support the local rural poor, identified strategies and implemented programmes, that strengthened their capacities and enabled them to address the issues of environmental degradation and to improve their social and economic conditions in a sustainable manner.

Palanithurai's paper on "*Role of youth in governance at grassroots*"[9] has enumerated a whole range of 24 village activities, which Gram Sabha members relying on youth, can perform. The point to be noted is that the activities mentioned here have been *operationalised in 54 Gram Sabhas in Tamil Nadu,* with the assistance of youth clubs and mahila mandals, which is a tremendous achievement. The Bhoovigyan Vikas Foundation, recently experimented with a pilot project in Uttaranchal State[10] by selecting a village cluster and organising the village youth by capacitating and training them in the various tasks of village planning. The involvement of youth (both men and women) in this project was very encouraging.

The most important question is how to make such developments self-sustaining. An analysis of the planning and management of the activities by some successful local group interns (in selected institutions in South and South-east Asian countries) and of their participatory and self-reliance character, conducted by the Asian and Pacific Development Centre at Kuala Lumpur (Malaysia), points to the importance of the following critical organisational variables viz.

1. Motivating factors
2. Group characteristics
3. Leadership
4. Programme thrusts, and
5. Management Style

(Khalid Shams, 1989)[11]

Voluntarism and its Emergence as our Civilisational Ethos

For a vast country with more than 700 million people in six lakhs villages like India, what is needed is "*Rural Renaissance through voluntarism*", which has to be orchestrated through Panchayati Raj, Gram Sabha, and Democratic Culture, to transform the existing mind-set of the people and implement the various programme initiatives of our present Government for Rural Development. This will lead to a healthy cooperation and integration of state-directed and voluntary initiatives. The current focus of our national government is on the following rural development programmes:

(i) Bharath Nirman for unlocking Rural India's Development potential through infrastructure creation;
(ii) National Rural Employment Guarantee Scheme;
(iii) The Sarva Shiksha Abhiyan;
(iv) The Mid-Day Meal Scheme;
(v) Rural Electrification and
(vi) Rural Road Schemes.

All the above programmes, along with the PURA Model*, advocated by our Hon'ble President[12], must fall in place through a broader networking of issues and by mainstreaming the village youth, empowered through a massive capacitation training programme. Here, we emphasise the need for the emergence of *vcluntarism* as our *civilisational ethos* and as an alternative model of development, with a strong advocacy for people's rights and entitlements, besides welfare and development.

---

* The President in his Address to the 93rd Science Congress has cited three examples: Periyar Pura in Tamil Nadu, Chitrakoot in Madhya Pradesh and Loni in Maharashtra. In all these models, Science and Technology has played important roles. He has called for a time-bound establishment of 100 Pura clusters and its components to achieve sustainable rural development through science and technology. These should be developed by 100 selected educational institutions or colleges, spread across the country with Rs. 500 crore funding.

Community Action Planning Paradigm through Nation-wide Action Group of Voluntary Youth

The Bhoovigyan Vikas Foundation held in Hyderabad during November 10-12, 2005, an International Conference on "*Rural India: Achieving Millennium Development Goals and Grassroots Development*". This stimulated one of its Fellow Members, Prof. Amarnath Kshathriya*, to float a proposal for the formation of a "*Nation-wide Action Group of Educated Youth*", called "*Scientists/ Engineers/Researchers/Vikasis/In Society*" *(SERVIS-INDIA)*[13] to help evolve a vibrant rural India, that will nurture the principles of Panchayati Raj and to develop a critical mass of youth (Vikasis) from urban and rural India, who will accelerate the building of a vibrant Rural India and help inaugurate a civil society with robust democratic values.

"*The Vikas Sainanis*" will be coalition builders between the members of the Gram Sabha and the Scientists/Engineers/Researchers in public sector with specified responsibilities for rural development (both in building up its physical infrastructure and Human Resource Development). With the assistance of District Government functionaries responsible for administration, and the local MLA and MP, they will function as catalysts to act as facilitators of social change in the rural community.

Prof. Kshatriya's idea of SERVIS can be stretched further by establishing mutual collaboration with scientists from Krishi Vigyan Kendras and Polytechnics and trained village youth, all of whom will constitute a "*Multi-layered paradigm of participatory youth Brigade*," (*See* Fig. 1) working for the common cause of Rural Renaissance. In this participatory paradigm, the Educated Youth (SERVIS) will form the top layer, who will provide the scientific and technological support, as well as the key ideas for strategic planning. They will prepare a comprehensive model of village planning, incorporating the aspirations and efforts of the local community, so that it might be grounded concretely in their own future. Apprehensions may

---

* Prof. Kshathriya, who is a Canadian citizen, has initiated the SERVIS programme in Canada with success and he is trying to operationalise it in his ancestral village in Jaunpur district in UP. E-mail: amar.kshatriya@telus.net

be raised as to how this can be made to happen. In my view, this is quite possible, if the student power in the universities is fully harnessed, with their teachers also providing the necessary input and guidance*. To enable this, it should be made mandatory for all graduate students in every discipline—Physical sciences, Social sciences, Engineering, Technology and Management—to spend the final six months of their education in rural service, studying the potentials and needs of a selected village cluster of about 20 villages, at the end of which they will prepare a report laying out an "*Operating Vision*" for the village cluster comprising four sections, *viz.*,

(1) Locating the underlying contradictions in the village cluster, which constitute the major deterrents to human progress in the villages.
(2) Making some practical proposals, which can overcome the observed deterrents.
(3) Outlining the tactical systems, indicating the practical actions necessary to initiate social change in the community, and
(4) Drawing up a shelf of projects with some programmatic details, which can bring about social and economic change in the community.

The second layer of this paradigm will comprise of the unemployed village youth with some school education (including school drop-outs), who can be trained in some specific skills to become social animators. They may be absorbed in the on-going Anganwadi programme, as social workers by suitably strengthening and restructuring the programme itself, as needed. The necessary funds for this purpose may be met from the Centre's National Employment Programme.

---

* In the mid-1930's, the land use and land cover maps for the entire country of Great Britain were prepared using student power, through the motivation and commitment of a Professor of Geography in the University of London, Prof. Dudley Stamp. Those were days, when such refined tools like Remote Sensing and Satellite Imageries were not available.

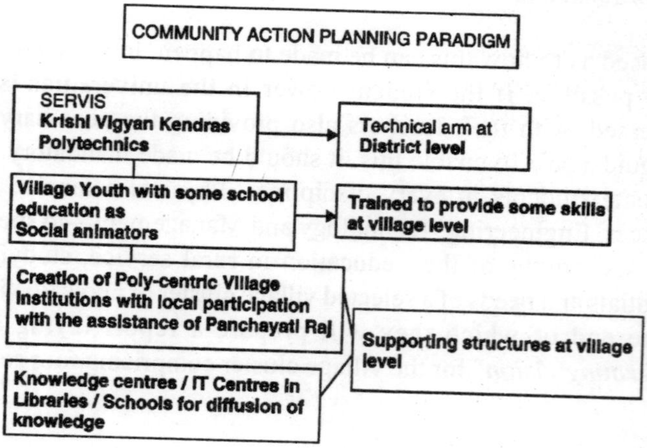

Fig. 1.1

The third component of the paradigm is "Organisation building", in which the Panchayati Raj institution in each village should play a crucial role by creating Poly-centric village institutions, with local participation such as User Groups, Self-help groups, Cooperatives, Women's groups etc. to act as a 'support network', and to interact with the public sector at the tahsil, district, state and national levels. If properly organised, their "ignition potential' will be indeed great.

The fourth component of this paradigm will be the setting up of "Knowledge Centres/IT centres in village Libraries/schools" for diffusion of knowledge, about which a lot is now being talked about. (Madaswamy Moni, 2005)[14].

If the above paradigm, involving both indigenous and outside participation, could be operationalised providing for the integration of local subjectivity and external objectivity, it will generate the momentum, energy and discipline needed for sustainable rural development.

Village Economic Resurgence through an Auto-Kinetic Model of Development

On the economic front, the effort should be to increase the recycling—ratios of village produce and to enhance the value added income of the village and to provide for the necessary "*connectivities*", "*flows*" and "*iterative interactions*" with the external communities and link the production, processing and marketing of the local produce.

The Bhoovigyan Vikas Foundation has prepared a model of Auto-Kinetic Model of Development, for creating an economically viable agricultural and industrial base for the village, and to initiate a process of engineering the overall development of productive forces with the objective of better satisfying the basic livelihood and the material needs of the rural population, based as far as possible on a more intensive utilization of local resources, by means of appropriate technologies[15]. The model of Auto-kinetic development may be seen in the following figure.

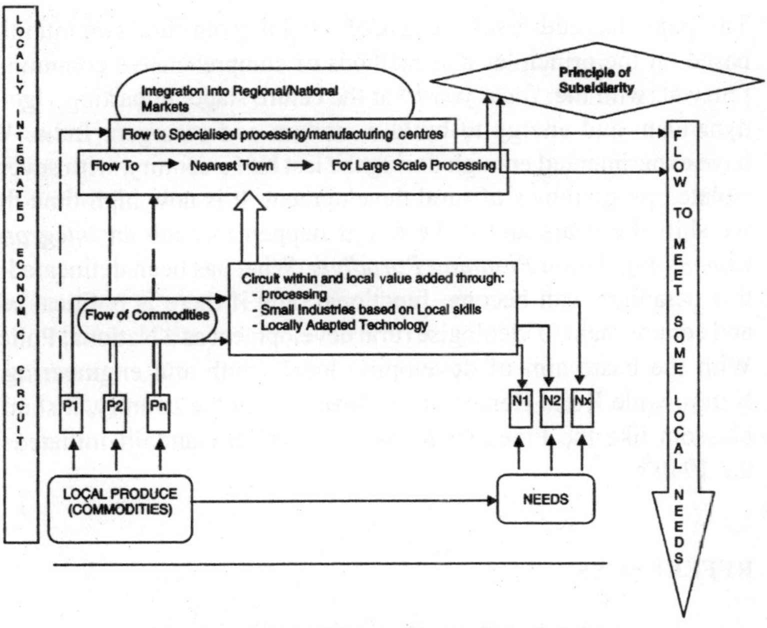

Fig. 1.2: Model of Autokinetic Development

For promoting cottage and small scale industries based on local resources, in this model, some technology input and technical assistance should be made available to youth for project planning and implementation. The existing Krishi Vigyan Kendras in the country, whose functions are at present limited to agro-related administration, can take on the role as technical support centres, by enlarging their functions and activities, thus imparting training in rural technologies for productive employment. Alternately, if local NGO's with some skills are available in the area, they can assist the gram sabhas and village youth in planning and implementation of development programmes with appropriate technologies. For upgrading their skills, Regional Polytechnics can conduct periodical training courses. In this way, a gradual transition could be effected. This is in other words, the adaptation and upgrading of existing facilities through the use of known appropriate technologies.

Summing up

This paper has addressed the task of reshaping our rural communities based on the principles and methods of comprehensive community renewal, with the *'local youth'* at the centre stage, imparting vigour, dynamism and energy to build a modern and resurgent India. We have experimented enough during the last half a century, with several isolated programmes of rural development. It is now high time that we shift the gears and make things happen through an *integrated Community Action Planning Paradigm*. What has been delineated in this paradigm, can become functional only if there is political will and commitment to ideologise rural development as a National Policy. With the basic aim of developing local youth and engineering a Nation-wide Rural Renaissance Movement in the country, it should blossom like the Freedom Movement, which Gandhiji initiated in the 1940's.

REFERENCES

1. Gautam Mathur, Effective Instruments for Equitable Transformation, Chapter 4 in "*Commonalities, Complementarities and Cooperation*", Association of Development Research and Training Institutes of Asia and the Pacific (ADIPA), 1989.
2. Khalid Shams, New approaches for Decentralised Rural Development—cases of Local Initiatives in Asia and the Pacific—Chapter 12 in "*Commonalities, Complementarities and Cooperation*", 1989.
3. Sundaram, K.V. : Decentralised Planning in the context of the New Panchayati Raj System in "*Emerging Trends in Panchayati Raj in India*"—S.P. Jain and Thomas W. Hochgesang. Published by National Institute of Rural Development, 1995.
4. Sundaram, K.V., Development from Within—A Rethinking on an Alternative Development Path, Asia-Pacific Journal of Rural

Development, Vol. IV, Nos. 1 and 2 (July and December, 1994).

5. State Planning Commission, Chennai: "*Report of the Working Group on Decentralised Planning and Panchayati Raj*" Oct. 1997, The author was the Chairman of the Working Group.
6. Planning Commission (Govt. of India): Towards Improved Local Level Planning for Rural Development—Lessons from some experiences, 1986. The author led the Evaluation team to study Kundrakudi development.

6a. Sundaram K.V. : Development from Within, (Chapter 5) and Chemistry of Micro-level Development (Chapter 6) in "*Decentralized Planning—Principles and Practice, Asian and African Experiences*" Concept Publishing Company Pvt. Ltd, New Delhi 1997.

7. Srikumar Chattopadhyay, "*Towards Gram Swaraj: West Bengal and Kerala Experiments*", ANASAKTI, Volume 1, No. 1, January 2003, International Centre for Gandhian Studies and Research, Gandhi Smriti and Darshan Samiti, Rajghat, New Delhi.
8. Vasantha Kumaran, T, Bala Hyma and David Wood, "*Community Action Planning*", T.R. Publications Ltd, PMG Complex First Floor, 8, South Usman Road, T. Nagar, Chennai-600017, 2004.
9. Palanithurai G, "*Role of youth in Governance at Grassroots*", Endeavour, Vol. 1, No. 1, July-December 2005, Rajiv Gandhi National Institute of Youth Development, Sriperumbudur-602105, Tamil Nadu.
10. Bhoovigyan Vikas Foundation, "*Devising Analytical Packages for Sustainable Natural and Human Resources Development for Decentralised Planning*", 2006 (Mimeograph).
11. Khalid Shams *Ibid*, 1989
12. A.P.J. Abdul Kalam, "*Dynamics of Rural Development*" Address at the 93rd Indian Science Congress, Hyderabad, 05-01-2006, www.presidentofindia.nic.in
13. Amarnath Kshatriya, "*Empowering Rural Youth with SERVIS*"—Theme Paper presented to the 3rd International Conference on "*Rural India, Achieving Millennium Development Goals and Grassroots Development*", Bhoovigyan Vikas Foundation, 2005.
14. Madaswamy Moni, "*Mainstreaming ICT for fostering Agricultural Growth, Poverty reduction and sustainable resource use to usher in rural prosperity*", Theme paper presented to the 3rd International Conference on "*Rural India, Achieving Millennium Development goals and grassroots Development*", Bhoovigyan Vikas Foundation, 2005.
15. Sundaram K.V. : "*Releasing the capillary Mechanisms for a Convergent Approach to Participatory Local Area Development*" in "*Reinventing Regional Development*"—Surya Kant, *et al.* (Edrs), Rawat Publications, Jaipur and New Delhi, 2004.

2

Beyond PURA and Towards the Next Phase of Rural Renaissance

I. Introduction

In order to conceive a well-balanced model of rural development, economically, socially and environmentally, the Government of India hopes to evolve an Action Plan for making the Tenth Plan, a *People's Plan,* and Development, a *People's Movement*. The programme announced for attaining this objective is through the establishment of *Knowledge Powered Village Complexes*, known by the acronym "*PURA*". (Provision of Urban amenities in Rural Areas). This is a key element of "Vision 2020" and is intended to give a new thrust to the all-round development of *viable village complexes* through the twin strategies of '*Effective Planning and Implementation of Rural Development Programmes with People's Participation*' and '*Effective Development Communication for People's Participation*'. The programme PURA is essentially a *Habitat Design* to achieve prosperous, peaceful and safe human habitat in rural areas that would improve the quality of life in rural places and lead to "*Inclusive Rural Development*".

The objective of this paper is to set the PURA Concept in the wider context of Holistic Village Cluster Development Planning to

---

* Key Note Address Delivered in The 3rd International Conference on "Rural India-Achieving Millennium Development Goals and Grassroots Development" 10-12th November, 2005 at Hyderabad.

achieve "Inclusive Development". Given the initial push for the vision by the President of India, what is needed today is nothing less than spearheading a nationwide *Village Renewal Movement,* based on a wider understanding of the PURA concept.

II. Why A Village Cluster?

In our present development context, the Indian village, with its small population, has ceased to be an economic and social entity for planning. The knowledge century demands a size suitable for the effective transfer of technology. Besides, people would want higher forms of services and of quality in provisions like health, education, agricultural inputs and services etc.

There is therefore, a need to think in terms of '*viable unit areas of development in rural space*'. It is in this context that the concept of a 'cluster of village' comes as a useful grassroots level unit for planning, for organizing rural development programmes. It is not a new idea and has been discussed, since the middle of the 1960's, though no concerted efforts were made to operationalize the approach. Now, with the PURA concept gaining ground, there has been a revival of interest on this approach to micro-level planning.

III. Evolution of the Concept

A review of the evolution of the thinking on 'village cluster approach' and of its relevance and usefulness as a tool for rural development would be a useful beginning to this discussion.

An early recognition of the concept was, when the First Master Plan for Delhi was prepared under the guidance of Albert Mayer of Etawah community development fame. The Delhi Master Plan adopted a hierarchical pattern of central villages, service centres and rural towns (based on Christaller's concept), for the limited purpose of bridging the rural-urban gap in the provision of social services[1]. A more concrete beginning towards this approach commenced when the Ford Foundation initiated in 1969, a *Pilot Research Project on Growth Centres* in collaboration with Govt. of India, envisaging a 'village cluster', around an identified growth centre, as an intermediate areal unit between the village and the block. It followed the typical spatial-cum-regional planner's approach of identifying a hierarchy of service centres (based on techniques like scalogram analysis), for extending a broad range of amenities, services and infrastructure to all settlements in the block. Thereafter, the sectoral scenarios of development are developed for agriculture, industry, education, health and transport to create an integrated spatial plan of development. This approach was also recommended by the Working Group on Block Level Planning, set up by the Planning Commission in 1978.[2]

Around the same time, an International Organization—The United Nations Research Institute for Social Development (UNRISD), Geneva, initiated research studies to examine the relevance of 'Growth Poles and Growth Centres' for regional development in the developing countries. We (Prof. R.P. Misra and myself) undertook a prestigious project funded by this organization to test the relevance of this concept in a most underdeveloped area of India. This led to our field study in 1963 in the Bastar district of Madhya Pradesh, a most backward tribal district. After this experience, we returned with rich insights and boldly stated our conviction that what are required to stimulate developments in such areas are "*Social Development Poles*", and '*People Centred Development*', rather than 'Growth Poles'. We viewed with great skeptism, the nature of '*modern*' developments taking place in the area by external agencies, e.g. the Bailadilla iron ore mining-developments, which were sweeping the economy of the tribals, '*off their feet*'.[3]

From the above experience stems our criticism about the mechanistic methodology, promoted through the spatial-cum-sectoral strategy, advocated by the growth pole researchers which, while using sophisticated criteria for determining the status of settlement centres (e.g. 'Population Threshold', Distance Norms', and Movement of People and Commodities'), blatantly ignored the inter and intra community relations in lower and grassroot level settlements and insights derived from the perception of rural contrasts and uneven economic and social development.

Since the 70's, the concept of rural development has undergone many changes. It is now "*Inclusive Socio-economic Development*", which inheres in it, the tasks of 'poverty reduction', 'employment generation', 'empowerment', 'equity', 'sustainable development of the natural resources', besides the provision of basic minimum services. It has *to be generated from* "*within*", by unleashing the "*Capillary Mechanisms*" in the village situation, with people deciding their course of development and government supporting it. In this conception, the core tasks of rural development will include the fuller use of land and water resources without destruction, modernization of farming by extending processing and marketing activities, building non-farm and allied agricultural activities, setting up institutions like cooperatives and other forms of social capital, empowering panchayats and women and improving health and education services. We, therefore argue, that in order to bring about '*Inclusive Rural Development, with people's participation nexus*', the growth impulses need to be structured and built up at the level of "clusters of villages", in a highly integrated and effective manner. This line of reasoning implies a new perspective and a much deeper '*economic and social content*', of development addressed to both policy delivery and receiving sides. It is much more than ensuring merely a viable size of settlement for supporting a particular amenity or service. In this conception, the effectiveness of a 'cluster' at grassroot level depends not so much on the size alone of the population brought together, but on the degree of cohesiveness and integration among the constituent villages and social groups, quality of local leadership and capacity of rural institutions to bring the rural weak and poor within their fold. It is here that understanding the village as a part of rural neighbourhood assumes importance in planning for development. This new concept of rural development can be translated into action only through 'social animators' (committed NGO's) and 'change agents' (researchers) joining hands with local bureaucracy/technocracy and local people and their institutions. It has to be seen as a *joint endeavour* of various "*Partners in Progress*", with clear goals. (Fig. 2.1: *Village Cluster Planning: Partners and Processes)*

IV. The Delineation of Village Clusters

The first initiating step for creating "*Inclusive Socio-economic Development in the Rural Areas*" would be the delineation of '*Village Clusters* (VCs)' as the grassroot level units for rural planning and development. The ideal rural planning units would be the "*Cohesive Rural Community*", which can be delineated by taking into account the social, economic and spatial inter-relationships, as well as the power structure of the community. The Village Clusters (VCs) are

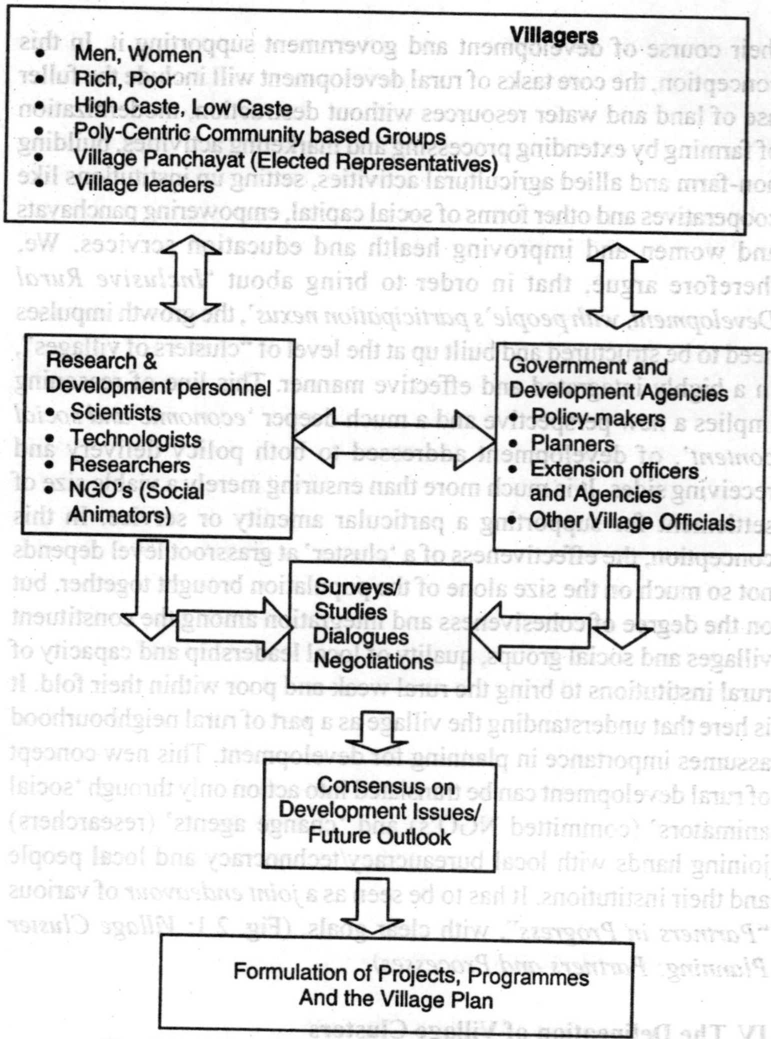

Fig. 2.1: Village Planning—Partners and Processes

thus envisaged as '*Community of Interest Areas* (CIAs)', in which people's association and social contacts will be of a voluntary nature, with people being drawn together by common interests in economic affairs, trade, social interests for recreation or religion etc. The focal point for each 'Community of Interest Area (CIAs)' will be a '*central place*' of viable population size, already performing some area-wide functions such as, school services, medical services, retail services, social and recreational services, business services and transport services. In order to delineate the hinterland of the selected central place, the analysis could proceed both from quantitative data available from secondary sources (e.g. for education and medical services), and combining this with enquiries made in the surrounding villages, so as to obtain a correct knowledge of those rural settlements, which customarily obtained a particular service from the given central place. Such investigations, coupled with the local knowledge of the relative "*pulls*" of the central places and the transport orientation and consumer travel patterns, will help to determine the hinterland of the selected central places. Mapping of "*Desire Lines*" for selected services in the rural areas may also be useful. With such methods, decisions about the central places and their hinterlands could be taken with a reasonable degree of accuracy.

Some of the studies made in micro-level planning in our country have concluded that a viable Village Cluster, which would be the lowest area level unit for planning and development, may cover 5-6 contiguous villages, having a distance span of 4-6 kms and with a total population of about 8,000-10,000. One of our important Committees on Panchayati Raj, which studied the optimum size of the rural unit for planning and development has also concluded that "a large size of rural unit should be appropriate for the villager's own interest for input supplies and provision of services like hospitals and schools, ware housing facilities, availability of higher order technical services and a host of other inter related functions, which forms part of the design of rural life" (Asok Mehta Committee, 1978).[4]

V. PURA in its Wider Context

The case for Village Clusters (VCs) as grassroots level units for planning and development has been made in the previous paragraphs. The VC is only a structural component of rural development. We may now consider as to how to make it a really '*functional unit*', surging with dynamism and activities. In the '*structural plan*' that has been unfolded with the '*central place*' as the '*hub*' or '*node*', and with the constituent villages as the different '*spokes*', dynamism has to be infused through various human activities. Here comes the PURA concept to our aid, as a tool to infuse the 'nodes', with various forms of 'connectivities', 'flows', and 'iterative interactions'.

'*Nodes*' are 'Nodal/Focal' points, which are endowed with a certain minimum threshold of population, infrastructure and services, and which have the potential to propel activities relevant to development and radiate development impulses to surrounding villages.

The four critical '*connectivities*' to induce development are: (i) *Physical Connectivity* or road and transport and power connectivity to bridge distances; (ii) *Electronic Connectivity* to increase communication through media and digital opportunities; (iii) *Knowledge Connectivity* through education and imparting of skills and extension services to provide information, technology, and increased understanding; and (iv) *Market Connectivity* to link rural products to markets. The inadequate presence of these connectivities have been seen as the "*major irritants*", or obstacles to development in our rural areas and their removal is considered vital for rural transformation.

Simply providing connectivities will not do. They should be rendered *dynamic* through '*flows*', which have to be consciously induced in four directions viz. vertical, downward, horizontal, and circular. The '*Vertical Flows*' will provide bottom-up connectivity to higher order centres of activity for processing of commodities produced in primary villages and information on local needs and preferences, area priorities, targets, local problems and constraints. The '*Downward or Top-down Flows*' will provide macro-micro linkages and information flows relating to policies, priorities, targets, guidelines, budgetary and technical support. '*Horizontal Flows*' will establish inter and intra community information flows and interactions. '*Circular Flows*' will enhance the recycling-ratio within the villages, adding income to the village and bringing about a circular movement of commodities from the primary villages to their processing centres and the return movement of finished products to consumer centres.

'*Interactions*' constitute the vital component of this dynamic system and is closely related to both electronic connectivity and knowledge connectivity. It involves (a) the interaction of the people's institutions with government's institutions; (b) the interaction of people, as individuals, with their own institutions, like the Village Panchayat and Community-Based Organizations (CBO's); and (c) people to people informal interactions through their social organizations.

Thus, the planning intervention envisaged as "*Cluster Development*" and sought to be operationalized here through the nodes, connectivities, flows, and interactions, in space will ensure participatory development and enable bridging the rural-urban gap, providing urban amenities in rural areas (PURA) and enhancing the quality of life and livelihood opportunities for the rural people.

VI. The Operating Vision, Tactics and Planning

"Where there is no vision, the people perish" is a well-known axiom. It is only with a clear operating vision of objectives, thrusts, tactics, and programmatic interventions that any Village Cluster (VC) can hope to meet its '*tryst with destiny*'. Initially such a vision will never be totally explicit. It is latent, as a community's attitude towards itself and its aspirations are not easily visible. With iterative interaction with different sections of the community, however, this can be discovered with some clarity. With the modern tools of analyses, the vision that is latent could be objectified.

Tactical Planning

The discussion on 'Nodes', 'Connectivities', 'Flows' and 'Interactions' presented in the fore going paragraphs relate to the rebuilding of fundamental community structures for the *Holistic Village Cluster Development Planning* in a multilevel framework (Fig. 2.2). They provide a broad framework for tactical planning i.e. for developing the tactics required to shape the destiny of the village. Thus tactical planning will describe and rationally organize the practical actions required for socio-economic change in the rural areas. The major tactical areas representing the 'overarching tasks' to be accomplished include:

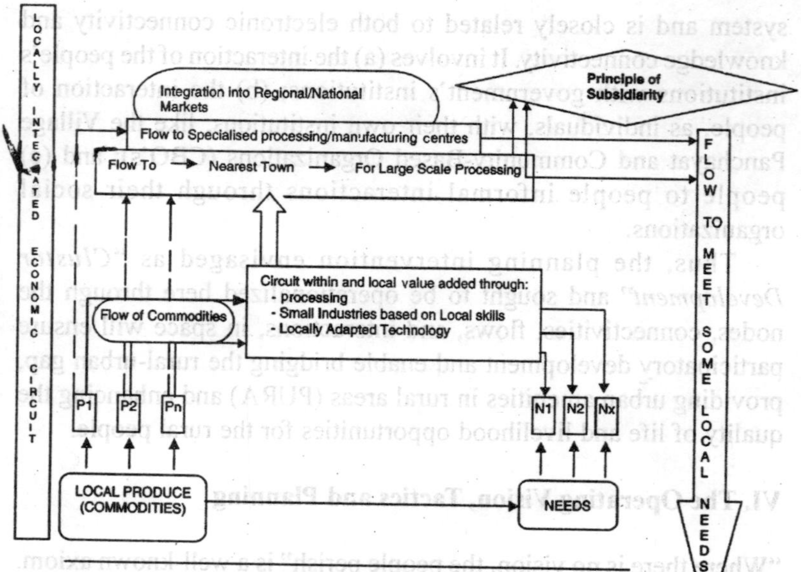

Fig. 2.2: Model of Auto-kinetic Development

Creating an economically viable agricultural and industrial base for the village on the lines of an Auto-kinetic Model of Development (Fig. 2.3). By auto-kinetic development, we mean a process by which the auto-centric and auto-dynamic forces of development can be unleashed, which will release the inner urges, potentials and energies inherent in the rural community. It is a process of engineering the overall development of productive forces, with the objective of better satisfying the basic livelihood and the material needs of the rural population, based as far as possible on a more intensive utilization of local resources, by means of locally adapted and locally controllable, labour-intensive and small-scale technologies. It is the same as the Gandhian concept of Village Swaraj or "Development from within", with the capillary mechanisms in place, but points to a definite method for augmenting rural incomes.

The auto-kinetic development process rests on the hierarchic principle of subsidiarity. That is, we seek to establish processing/ manufacturing units at higher level, only when the existing technologies and skills do not allow these to be performed in a satisfactory fashion and at a justifiable cost in the lower spatial level. In the auto-kinetic development approach, the basic objective of achieving the full development of the natural resources and human skills available in the villages can be secured only by establishing "locally integrated economic circuits"

The integrated economic circuit concept implies several other ideas such as engineering circular effects, chain effects and recycling the primary produce of the village into secondary lines of production. The Recycling Ratio is a measure of the extent of rural industrialization. Application of these concepts may lead to specialization and in some areas even to the establishment of a "territorial production complex".

Guarding the basic physical well-being of the village society by ensuring food and nutrition security, public health and sanitation and providing health care.

Developing functional life skills, including upgrading of basic practical literacy skills at all age levels and providing practical training in marketable business and crafts and providing access to agricultural services including inputs and markets.

Another tactical arena would be breaking the isolation of the village and establishing external support relations. This could be established through fostering the necessary institutional relations with the Public and Private sectors and adapting the development programmes initiated by the government, to suit the local specificities and needs, forging extended business contacts, e.g. for securing bank loans to fund local projects and promoting the village public image.

Leveraging Information and Communication Technology (ICT) is one of the major tactics for transforming the village into a knowledge-based society. This would call for establishing a "Knowledge Communication Centre (KCC)" and training the rural youth in computer literacy. In this manner, agricultural information for precision farming from extension agencies and price signals from neighbouring market centres could be accessed by the rural community. The 'Hub and Spoke Model' for a knowledge communication centre is illustratively indicated in Fig. 2.4.

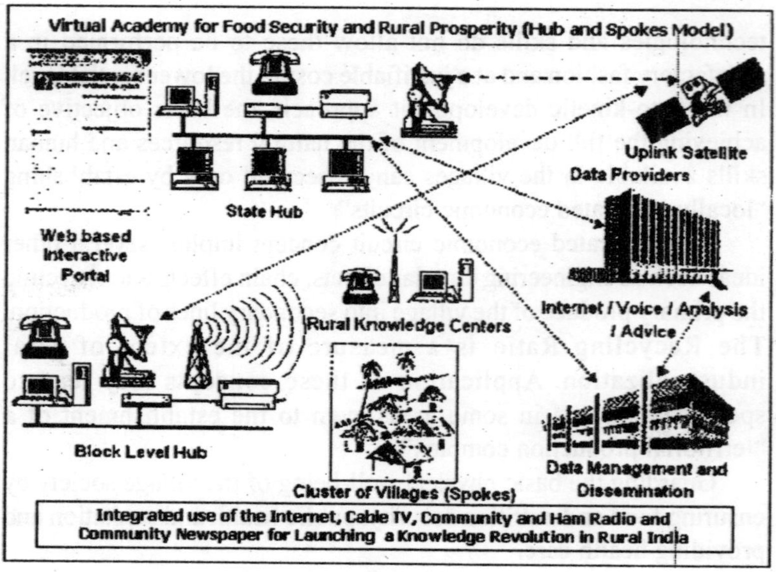

Fig. 2.3

The arching dimensions of the operating vision may be visualized in five broad groups viz. community sustenance; habitat improvement; sustainable development; institutional support; and social awakening. Each group has been further elaborated to indicate the major thrusts and further detailed into 'enabling programmatic interventions', for actuating the 'Vision'. These are outlined in Table-1, which illustrates in a nutshell the planning framework for the study.

Programme Content

Successful implementation of the Holistic Village Cluster Development strategy requires complex decentralized matrix structures, with permanent mechanisms for vertical and lateral integration, a combination of specialist and generalist skills, institutional leadership, social intervention capability and systems management. The methodology and programme content would include the building up of the databases for decision-making through secondary and primary surveys and selected studies conducted by using PRA methods. A seven-fold programmatic design is advocated which will aim at (1) Ensuring Sustainability of Resource Base

Table 1: Holistic Village Cluster Development Project: Operating Vision

Objectives (Broad Groups)	*Major Thrusts*	*Programmatic Interventions*
Community Sustenance (upgrading the economic foundations of village life)	1. Agri-Production Complex	Production and productivity increase, Transportation,Marketing and credit Linkages, product diversification
	2. Food and Nutrition Security	Grain Golas; and Effective PDS; Livestock/Poultry/Horticulture development
	3. Full Employment	SME's through Integrated Economic Circuit
Habitat Improvement	4. Village Reconstruction and provision of basic amenities	Housing rehabilitation, Public utilities and facilities, Power, communication and transport systems
Sustainable Development	5. Ecodevelopment (Biovillage)-Promoting conservation and job-led growth opportunities.	Land and Water Management; biodiversity conservation
Institutional Support	6. Poly-centric Planning and Management Institutions	Village Planning Forum, Village Skill Development Centre, Village Knowledge and Communication Centre Cooperatives, User Groups, And CBO's.
Social Awakening	7. Social Rebuilding (through social animators)	Training and education for social effectivity, Literacy training, Training for women/youth, Land Army, Barefoot Doctors/Engineers/Technologists etc.

(ii) Poverty Alleviation, (iii) Empowerment of Women, (iv) Full Employment, (v) Production Systems Planning, (vi) Infrastructure Planning and (vii) Habitat Planning. These are further elaborated in the accompanying Flow Chart (Fig. 2.5). The Bhoovigyan Vikas Foundation hopes to seek to translate the operating vision elucidated in this paper into a few pilot projects in different typological areas.

The operating vision for rural development outlined in this paper and many of its underlying concepts bear a close imprint of Mahatma Gandhi's vision for the reclaiming of the rural villages across our country.

VII. Expected Outputs

There will be the following major outputs from this project.

1. It will establish a methodology for "Micropolitan-centred Village Cluster Development" in a participatory-cum-research action mode, with the Panchayati Raj institutions, Village Leaders, Community-based Organisations, NGO's and a Team of Researchers joining hands in a common endeavour of village development through social mobilization.
2. It will initiate a village development movement in the country through auto-kinetic processes aimed at a pro-nature, pro-poor, pro-employment and pro-women development paradigm of sustainable agriculture and rural development.
3. The project will enable a critical mass of village youth to be trained in planning and implementation of rural development activities.
4. It will enable the Ministry of Rural Development, Government of India to issue appropriate Guidelines on Village Development Planning to the State Governments.

This exercise will be a valuable input to the formulation of village action programmes during the 10th Five Year Plan in respect of operationalising micro-level planning at the grassroots level, all over the country through the Panchayati Raj Institutions and other "partners in progress" and initiating a "Rural Renaissance Movement" in the country.

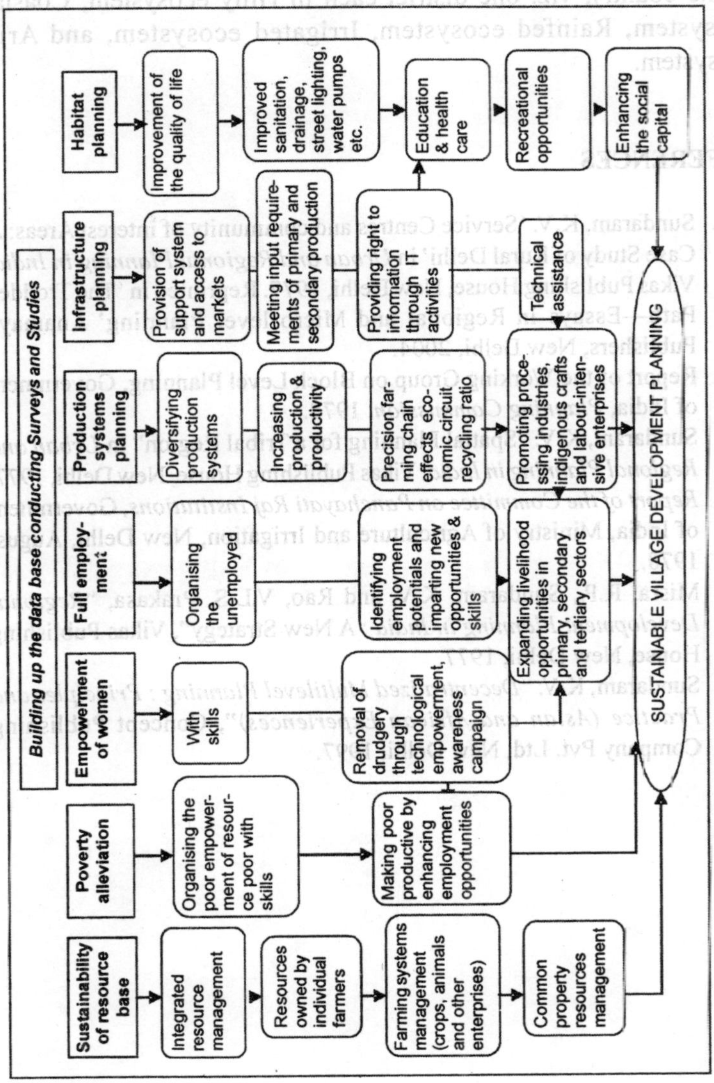

Fig. 2.4: Holistic Planning for a Village Cluster: Concepts and Key Dimensions

VIII. The Project Sites

The project is proposed to be undertaken in all the five ecosystems of the country, viz. one district each in Hilly ecosystem, Coastal ecosystem, Rainfed ecosystem, Irrigated ecosystem, and Arid ecosystem.

REFERENCES

1. Sundaram, K.V. 'Service Centres and community of interest Areas: A Case Study of Rural Delhi' in *Urban and Regional Planning in India*, Vikas Publishing House, New Delhi, 1977. Reprinted in 'The Trodden Path—Essays in Regional and Micro-level Planning' Anamaya Publishers, New Delhi, 2004.
2. Report of the Working Group on Block Level Planning, Government of India, *Planning Commission*, 1978.
3. Sundaram, K.V. "Spatial Planning for a Tribal Region" in *Urban and Regional Planning in India,* Vikas Publishing House, New Delhi, 1977.
4. *Report of the Committee on Panchayati Raj Institutions*, Government of India, Ministry of Agriculture and Irrigation, New Delhi, August 1978.
5. Misra, R.P., Sundaram, K.V. and Rao, V.L.S. Prakasa, "*Regional Development Planning in India* : A New Strategy", Vikas Publishing House, New Delhi, 1977.
6. Sundaram, K.V. "*Decentralized Multilevel Planning : Principles and Practice (Asian and African Experiences)*", Concept Publishing Company Pvt. Ltd, New Delhi, 1997.

II
Regional/Area Development

3

Regional Planning: An Analysis in Retrospect and Prospect

Recently, an old colleague of mine posed a question to me. "Between 1960s and 1980s, there used to be a lot of discussion about Regional Planning. But now there is no talk about it. Does it mean that Regional Planning is dead?" I replied: "So long as spatially unbalanced development, manifested in depressed regions, backward areas, primate cities, environmentally degraded areas, poverty and unemployment pockets, out-migration areas, derelict regions, industrially backward areas, regions undergoing major resource development projects involving population shifts etc. exist, regional planning will also exist with necessary conceptual retooling, mutations and adaptations in new forms or '*Avatars*', and perhaps with new titles too. However, the basic doctrine i.e. "spatially oriented thinking" remains the same." I added that now, in the expression 'Regional Planning', the term 'region' represents merely a taxonomic category, a functional sub-unit of national space.

I thought, I will begin this keynote address with these observations to emphasize the point that several paradigmic shifts in regional planning have taken place in our planning history to meet the challenges of our changing times.

---

* Key Note Address Delivered at the 26th National Geography Congress on 5-11-2004 at Maharishi Dayanand University, Rohtak (Haryana).

The theme that I am addressing to you today is on: '*Regional Planning—An Analysis in Retrospect and Prospect*'. It will deal with the evolution of Sub-national Planning or Regional Planning in our country and the next steps indicating the overwhelming developmental imperatives in our present context. Right from the time we gained our Independence in 1947, we have gone through more than half a century of planning experience, packed with events, and Sub-national Planning has taken various forms or '*Avatars*'. In this process, undoubtedly we have experimented with different types of '*Area Planning*' and gained rich experience.

I am not going to narrate the full story, as it is a long and winding one. But I shall certainly hit at some high spots of our experience.

The Post-independent De-Colonization Phase: Top-down Planning

The new Nation commenced its journey towards development in the 1950's with a grand vision, held out by our founding fathers during the freedom struggle. We began in a highly optimistic mood to construct an economically strong and socially just society. The most pertinent question that arose at that time was "*what should be the areal units for planning*". It was a stage of conceptual confusion with conflicting views. Nevertheless, intellectually, it was an interesting period with a lot of arguments, counter-arguments, debates, agreements and disagreements, and more than all these, followed by some research experimentations also.

Resource-based Regionalisation

The first advocacy was towards '*Resource-based Regionalisation*' of the country. This concept inherited the thinking of the Soviet experience on identifying the "*Resource-driven Propulsive Activities*" and building '*Territorial Production Complexes*'. This led to the formulation of alternative models of '*Economic Regions*' for the country, in which a number of academics, particularly geographers, made valuable contributions.

Planning Regions to Bridge Inter-state Disparities

At a later stage, a concept of '*Group of States Planning Regions*' was advocated, this time by a government department, the Town and Country Planning Organisation, of the Government of India, which advocated the idea of '*Inter-state Regions*'[1] together with relevant regional policies to bridge the Inter-state disparities in development. A Regional Planning experiment with this slant was carried out in a region, carved out in the Coal-Steel belt of India, called the "South-east Resource Region", as a collaborative exercise with the concerned state governments, which is all well known to you. It was a unique effort, '*a work of some awesome earnestness*', as I termed it in my R.N. Dubey Memorial Lecture delivered at Allahabad in 1999.[2] It provided an excellent illustration of collective decision-making in the federal context, with the participating states joining the venture in a sprit of collaboration and cooperation. In spite of its intrinsic merits, this Inter-State Regional Planning did not take roots. I am not going into the reasons for the failure.

In any case, the search for a new spatial order for planning did not lead us anywhere. We finally accepted the linguistic '*States*', as planning units and moved on with our planning experiments in a '*two tier-federalism*".

Decentralisation of Planning—First Phase

That brings us to the first stage of decentralization of planning. If there is a moment in the history of development planning in our country, which I can actually pin-down as the *most significant,* that moment is the year 1969—the beginning of the Fourth Five Year Plan, when the first phase of Decentralization from top-down planning to the state level materialized. Significantly, the Fourth Five Year Plan is regarded as the "*Watershed*" in Indian Planning. With great determination, the Planning Commission brought about new procedures for the allocation of central assistance in order to share functions and finances with the states and encourage them to independently plan for their territories according to their own needs and priorities.

Area-Specific Planning Below State Level

This first stage of '*Decentralization*' led the state governments to build up their planning capabilities. At the same time, the Central Government, laid down some sectoral priorities through '*fund earmarking*' procedures. Further, in the interests of '*balanced regional development*', the centre initiated some area specific programmes, with focus on some "*Special Target Areas*" and "*Target Groups*". These collectively came to be known as the "*Development strategy for the development of selected backward areas*" in the country. Thus the planning for backward areas became another '*avatar*' of regional planning in the country. The three typologies of backwardness targeted in this context, were (a) areas characterized by past historical neglect—the typical '*bypassed areas*' in development, (b) areas affected by adverse factor endowments, e.g. adverse climate, difficult terrain conditions, degraded land areas and areas characterized by scarcity of water, and (c) areas characterized by social backwardness specially areas inhabited by tribals, marginalized groups and oppressed communities.[3] Thus began a phase of special programme planning for the hill areas, the tribal areas, the drought prone areas, the desert areas, the Western Ghats region, and the north-eastern region of the country, which marks the third shift of the Regional Planning Paradigm in the country.

Towards Multi-Level Planning

As this change towards Decentralised Planning in a two-tier federalism, with focus on backward areas development was in progress, in some states limited experimentations in building up democratic institutions below the state level were also tried. It was an inevitable development, as the states themselves felt the need for carrying out the decentralization process, down to a lower level, for reaching the people through some local institutional mechanisms, which can perform at least some agency functions. Thus block level planning and village level planning came to be advocated not merely as delivery mechanisms, but also with a modicum of planning functions to tackle the economic problems of poverty and unemployment at decentralised levels of administration. They later became the centrally sponsored programmes of poverty alleviation and employment generation. Simultaneously, in keeping with the changing paradigms in planning, the Indian Planning Commission also began advocating a two-way process of top-down and bottom-up planning through "*Multi-level Planning*". This meant a significant departure in the *style, stance* and *substance* of planning; '*style*' refers to the democratic and participatory character of planning; '*stance*' refers to the 'people doing and Government supporting a *two-way planning process*'; and '*substance*' refers to the programme and project components informed by the goals of growth, equity, stability and sustainability.[4] Among the developing countries in the world, the Indian Planning Commission was the first one to set-up a Multilevel Planning Division, which vigourously advocated the principles of Multilevel Planning.

Multilevel Planning, however was not a new idea for India. Gandhiji used the beautiful expression "*Planning in Oceanic Circles*" for this jargon, to describe the grassroots planning of his dream, which was contained in his agenda for establishing '*Self-reliant village Republics*' upwards. Later, the government approved a three-tier system of Panchayati Raj Institutions (PRI's), as recommended by the Balwantrai Mehta Study Team in 1958. The Panchayati Raj Institutions set up in many states during this period, worked as bureaucratically controlled, state funded delivery arms of the Government, with only a semblance of democratic set-up.

Towards Three-Tier Federalism and increased 'Localism' in Planning

This stalemate continued for a long time—as long as 35 years—till the 73rd and 74th Constitutional Amendments were passed in 1993, by the Indian Parliament, which led to the establishment of Local Self-Government institutions in the country. Thus the year 1993 is an important *cut off point* in the context of the evolution of local level planning in India.

The new status accorded to the Panchayati Raj Institutions by the Constitutional Amendments raised high hopes and expectations among the elected representatives and the rural folk at large. However, as many evaluation studies have shown, the achievements have been '*nominal*' or '*sub-optimal*'. In an appraisal of the achievements of "*Decentralised Planning and Financing of Rural Development in India*" carried out for a World Bank sponsored seminar in the Asian Institute of Technology, Bangkok in 1999, I concluded that "'*If*

Democratic Decentralization is viewed as a stages approach', it can be safely asserted that India has successfully crossed the first stage *i.e. enfranchisement*—and has partially moved with limited success towards the second stage *i.e. empowerment*. But what may be called the '*Third Wave of Democratic Transformation*', which is the '*Transparent and Ethical mode of functioning*' is yet to be addressed in its totality. This is a stage of consolidating democratic institutions, materializing a multilevel planning process and ensuring its effective functioning with some work ethics and managerial efficiency".[5] As I have seen in many Asian and African countries, this is a long drawn-out process, perhaps never realized to perfection. Further, it must be noted that any change or transformation in developing countries moves in tandem with economic and social change, which are necessarily long-term changes, but crucial to the successful implementation of decentralised planning policies. As we see today, the real vacuum in development in the developing countries of Asia and Africa is to be found *at the local level* in our rural areas.

In the present context of globalisation and liberalisation, the challenge is: how are we to steer the local development process at the grassroots level by promoting "*development from within*".[6] Here, it is the local level planning which holds the key. Thus the emphasis in Regional Planning today has to be on planning at the micro level, comprising of village clusters, development blocks, districts and groups of districts. It calls for creating a psychological climate for rural renaissance through participatory local planning.

Economic Reforms: and 'Externalities' Influencing Local Development

India's growth is believed to have accelerated in the 1990's in response to the economic reforms. There is also a growing consensus that the improved growth since 1981 reduced poverty, and reforms in the 1990's have increased the economic inequality in all its aspects.[7] Some studies to verify these propositions have however pointed out that there has not been much diffusion of growth; on the other hand, the trends are towards the polarization in the economy.[8] In the garb of addressing the issues in global partnership for achieving the '*Millennium Development Goals*', the developed countries are making the conditions more difficult for the developing countries, especially for their rural sector, by perpetuating a situation of permanently keeping them in '*Poverty Traps*'. This is the present international scenario.

Transforming Rural India: Micro-Level Planning

At home, a new government has taken over the reins of government and some fresh thinking is brewing. Our Prime Minister is calling for a new deal of *Rural India.* Our President is emphasizing on the *Provision of Urban Amenities in Rural Areas (PURA).* The Tenth Plan strategy is emphasizing the generation of rural employment. But how are we to achieve all that?

Transforming Rural India is a challenging task. In our current thinking, it has to be along a '*triple bottom line*' i.e. along economic, ecological and social fronts. To achieve such an inclusive development, we need the support of a '*Fusion or convergence of Technologies*', besides poly-centric institutional structures that can take our villages along the development path, *fast forward in time.*

There needs to be a total 'inversion' of the planning process, in which our villages, grouped into economically viable village clusters, can transform themselves into 'growth engines' and harness the latent power and resources of the village community. This will be possible through an Auto-Kinetic Model of Development Planning, engineered through participatory approaches as well as through the application of sophisticated technologies like Remote Sensing, GIS, GPS, Biotechnology, Green Technologies etc. During the last more than half a century of our 'Learning Curve', we tried to bring about rural development through a large number of loose and fragmented central and centrally sponsored schemes handed down from above. But the very large number of such schemes and the organizational pluralism, which they entailed, encouraged corruption and spelt their total failure. The new approach to micro-level sub-national planning must address itself to five critical challenges, which are (a) poverty reduction; (b) employment and value added income generation at household, village, block and regional levels; (c) widely shared growth; (d) sustainable natural resource management through integrated water resource management and farmer-relevant land use planning strategy; and (e) strategic investments in people through education, health, connectivities and water supply and sanitation.

A model of rural development-an *Auto-kinetic Model*-conceptualized on these lines would be a very relevant one, which is now being discussed by intellectuals and planners in different quarters—the academia and those in the corridors of power. This model seeks to enhance farm productivity and income by aligning output with market demand through connectivities. Its primary focus would revolve around creating markets for local products and enhancing processing and secondary lines of production, thus helping to raise village incomes and the skills of the village youth as well as the entrepreneurial abilities of the local private sector. This model inheres the concepts of increasing recycling ratios in the village and augmenting the local economic circuit as well as the chain and linkage effects of development. I have outlined these concepts in my N.P. Ayyar Memorial Lecture delivered at the NAGI Conference 2001 at Sagar University.[9] This is a process of "Planning in Oceanic Circles". It is a process of linking production, processing and marketing systems. The Bhoovigyan Vikas Foundation has also prepared a Blue Print for such a model of development and is experimenting with it.

Before I conclude, I want to share with you two recent developments in the area of micro level planning. One is about the DISNIC programme, which the National Informatics Centre (NIC) had initiated in 1985. It has now been revived with the thrust on the applications of the data for rural development and grassroots governance. In this context, a major project involving Geography departments with institutional linkages to provide continuous planning support to development agencies in districts is being planned. The second is a massive programme for the development of 100 selected backward districts in the country, which the Planning Commission is launching.

These turn of events are expected to provide great opportunities to Geographers in this new century. It will be reinventing regional and local level planning with 'increased localism' and through an appropriate Technocratic, Academic and Democratic Mix (TAD Mix).[10] This will enable us to plan our villages with greater understanding and move from Vision to Action, towards a people-centred and people-driven movement of Rural Renaissance. It is my dream that Geographers will be in the forefront of this movement.

REFERENCES

1. Sundaram, K.V. 'From Top-down Planning to Decentralized Regional and Local Development in India', *Indian Social Science Review*, Vol. 2, No. 2, July-December 2000, Indian Council of Social Science Research, New Delhi.
2. Sundaram, K.V. "Planning Revisited: Rural Area Development in India-Vision and Reality"—3 Lectures published by *R.N. Dubey Memorial Foundation*, Allahabad, 2000.
3. Sundaram, K.V. "Search for Strategy: Regional Development and Planning for the Backward Areas in India"—Chapter Thirteen in "*Regional Development Alternatives*", A.L. Mabogunje (Eds.), Published by Maruzen Asia, Singapore: 1981 for the U.N. Centre for Regional Development, Nagoya (Japan).
4. Sundaram, K.V. "Multilevel Planning: Principles and Practice—Asian and African Experiences", Concept Publishing Company Pvt. Ltd, New Delhi, 1997.
5. Sundaram, K.V. "Decentralised Planning and Financing of Rural Development in India" (Reprinted)—in *Decentralization, Local Governance and Rural Development*. Ed. Hans Detlef Kammier and Harvey Demaine, *Proceedings of the International Workshop on Decentralized Planning and Financing of Rural Development in Asia*, January 1999, Published by Asian Institute of Technology, Bangkok, 2000.
6. Sundaram, K.V. "*Development from Within—A Rethinking on an Alternative Development Path*" in *Asia-Pacific Journal of Rural Development*, Volume IV, Nos. 1 and 2, July and December 1994, Centre on Integrated Rural Development for Asia and the Pacific, Dhaka.
7. Abhijitsen, Himanshu. "Poverty and Inequality in India Parts I and II"—Economic and Political Weekly, September 18 and 30, 2004.
8. Surya Kant, "Regional Pattern of Economic Development in Post-Reform India" in *Indian Social Science Review*, Vol. 4, No. 2, July-December 2002, Indian Council of Social Science Research, New Delhi.
9. Sundaram, K.V. "Rural Renaissance through a Spatially-Oriented Strategy of Development"—Prof. N.P. Ayyar First Memorial Lecture delivered in the 23rd Indian Geography Congress at the Dr. H.S. Gour University, Sagar (M.P.) India, Dec. 28, 2001
10. Sundaram, K.V. "Chemistry of Micro-level Development in Decentralized Multilevel Planning: Principles and Practice: Asian and African Experiences" Concept Publishing Company Pvt. Ltd., New Delhi, 1997.

4

Environmental Management, Locational Decisions and Regional Planning: The Case for the Development of the North-Eastern Region of India

Hon'ble Vice Chancellor, Prof. Mrinal Miri, Prof. Surendra Singh, Members of the Faculty of NEHU, Ladies and Gentlemen and friends.

The fact that you are holding this conference in a region experiencing rapid changes in resource transformation, population growth, transition from shifting cultivation, and problems in natural resources management, such as decline in environmental quality and loss of bio-diversity, makes it timely and relevant to ponder and discuss as to how our developmental approach to this region should reconcile ecology, economics and ethics and connect the broken links between them. The theme of the conference is one with three significant components of development viz. Environmental Management, Locational Decisions and Regional Planning. Regional Planning is the vital tool to development and environmental management as well as locational planning. In the preoccupation of the Central Government with the macro-planning issues of improving our balance of payments and correcting the fiscal deficit, the major responsibility for shouldering the tasks of sub-national planning and development now rests on the regional, state and local levels. These tasks have now to be performed on the basis of the "*subsidiary principle*". That is, what

---

* Chief Guest Address delivered in the International Conference held in the North Eastern Hill University, at Shillong During 5-9, March 2002.

can be done exclusively at each one of these levels must be done at those levels only. Thus a hierarchical, regional and local level planning, particularly involving environmental resources must become a complementary effort to national planning.

It is only through meticulous regional and local planning that the flexibility and creativity needed to counteract the present deadlock in our development process can be achieved. This approach to find the appropriate solution must be based on participatory and democratic procedures. In effect, it must be based on a strategy of decentralized planning through a process of auto-kinetic development or development from within. This alone will ensure our 'collective survival' in this new millennium of rapid change and development. Posited as we are, against the processes of globalization and liberalization of our economy, we need to look ahead, not only in the sense of anticipating what we can expect to happen, but also to lift our sights to lateral thinking, involving risk perception and the need to free ourselves from the trappings of a consumer-oriented and resource intensive mode of existence. I leave my musings on the regional and local philosophies of development and move on to other aspects.

The central issue, of the theme of this conference as I would like to put it, is how to manage our environmental resources, how to influence the locational decisions of some crucial 'region-forming' development projects for achieving better spread and multiplier effects, how to pursue a policy of openness in governance and how to opt for interdependence rather than independence in order to contribute to a positive effort towards the cultural integrity and economic integration of the region with the nation. All these, of course must be pursued with the basic objective of breaking out of the vicious cycles of poverty of the millions of our population, making them productive and harnessing their energies in nation-building tasks. I must admit to being very hesitant about making any forecasts or suggestions on these policy issues. That should realistically emerge from the intensive deliberations that you are going to have during these five days of your Conference. I must, however emphasize that at this juncture, when our 10th Five Year Plan is on the anvil, more and more cross-disciplinary dialogues and scientific discussions are necessary to find development alternatives to the various problems affecting our Common Future. Regional Conferences of this kind will help to diagnose the contradictions and dilemmas in our present approaches to development and provide concrete suggestions for more appropriate alternative development paths. I think, this is the best way to improve the understanding of our regional realities and move on towards better informed spatial strategies of development.

In this new century, by the term 'development', we mean a sustainable process, which is a holistic and integral process, as well as a value loaded and cultural process, encompassing the natural environment, social relations, education, production, consumption and human well being. The plurality of approaches or roads to development implied here, should be in response to the specificity of our cultural and regional situations. There can be no universal formula for development. It must emerge from endogenous endeavours and must spring from the heart of each society and region. It must be rooted on its own strength and resources. It must be based on the vision of its people, as determined by their needs and priorities and sharing their ideas and aspirations.

When I think of a region like the North East, rich in its indigenous and native culture, my thought runs to the need for respecting the specific cultures that are here, which bind human societies together. By 'culture' in this context, I mean not only the arts, literature or aesthetic canons of these societies, but most importantly their underlying codes of operation on which symbolism, ethical priorities, behaviour patterns and systems of knowledge are based. Given the harsh experiences of the past, we know that culture, as understood in this manner, is losing its role in the development philosophies of our belligerent world today. Sustaining our cultural diversity, with its traditional knowledge systems and symbolic representations, must be acknowledged as essential to the survival of our human civilization, by re-adapting and reinterpreting these 'ethno-sciences' in the light of new technologies. This is a vast subject in itself and I only make a passing reference to it here.

With this prelude, I come to some contextual aspects of our development problem. Here, I do not claim to any new thinking or radical new insights or proposals, but would like to repeat certain facts and arguments that may serve to concretize our developmental thinking and help in designing an area-specific action package. Our region here is a unique geographical entity in the country—a hill, forest and tribal economy, with abundant natural resources, rapidly marching towards progress. This state of 'Meghalaya' (this name was coined by the late Prof. S.P. Chatterjee, a doyen of Indian geography), as its very name implies is the presence of an abundance of water resources. Besides Meghalaya, all the other states in this region also are rich treasure-houses of natural resources, forest cover, biological and cultural diversity and with high ethnic plurality of human resources, inheriting rich indigenous knowledge systems. About a couple of decades ago, this region had comparatively lower population density, but of late, it has registered a higher growth rate of population, both as net natural growth as well as through cross-border in-migration. This has led to both insurgency and new environmental problems, leading to deforestation, loss of bio-diversity, land degradation as well as landslides, caused by some development activities like mining and construction of roads. There have also been illegal encroachment into forest areas, poaching of wild animals and smuggling of timbers and other forest products. I do not want to go into the various scientific, technological and legal aspects of overcoming these problems. Nevertheless, I understand that there are several traditional ways of forest and bio-diversity conservation methods practiced by the people of the North-East. I would like to emphasize that these practices should be preserved. I understand that this region is classified as one of the "*bio-diversity hot spots*" of the world. According to one source, it has at least 7,500 flowering plants, 700 orchids, 58 bamboo species, 64 citrus varieties, 28 conifers types, 500 mosses, 700 ferns and 728 lichen species. The region is also rich in faunal diversity. In this context, I would consider a systematic survey of the region's bio-diversity and its classification and assembly as an essential *pre-investment priority*. In any case, determined efforts should be made to conserve, manage and utilize this rich bio-diversity of the region by preserving its age-old traditional practices and carefully adapting them with such benign modern technologies, as are suitable.

Besides the problem of degradation of natural resources, to which I made a brief mention, the region also faces certain other problems like floods, which have been caused by both natural and anthropogenic factors. The flood problem has been a chronic one. It has to be tackled through both structural as well as non-structural methods. Watershed management, adoption of more ecologically suited land use patterns, including steady and phased withdrawal of *Jhum* cultivation practices, preventing reclamation of swamps and checking the encroachment into the marshy flood plain areas and reforestation are essential to contain the floods. Also, the system of flood forecasting, warning and management will need to be steadily strengthened with the kind of automated systems developed for the Brahmaputra and Barak valleys. Combined with storages and detention reservoirs, this could moderate the floods and reduce their duration, depth, extent of inundation and damage. The environmental damage caused by mining and the large dams constructed in this highly seismic zone, are the other man-made problems, that need to be carefully handled in the future development of this region.

The transition from shifting cultivation to settled agriculture is also an important issue to be handled with great care and caution. Modifying the existing cultivation practices suitably, keeping its adverse effects to the minimum, however, is a major problem. I understand that there are some new land use models such as Sloping Agriculture Land Technology (SALT) and Sloping Watershed Environmental Engineering Technology (SWEET) are some techniques which have been tried successfully.

You have rightly included 'locational aspect' as one of the essential theme components for discussion. This is rightly so, because the settlements of this region are of small population size lying in scattered hamlets, none of which is viable for the establishment of even elementary social infrastructure such as provision of educational institutions, healthcare and other social facilities. In this context, forced regrouping of settlements is not the appropriate solution. In many countries, where it was tried, it was a failure. On the other hand, we should go in for a functionally satisfying pattern of spatial planning, with a sprinkling of small growth points, growth centres and micropolises, linked to a cluster of hamlets through footpaths, footbridges, roads and other means of communication and providing the access to essential goods and services. Such a development should be fostered in consultation with local bodies and community-based institutions. Geographers who are traditionally trained in spatial theories and the use and application of spatial information technologies, like the GIS and LIS technologies, are specially equipped to handle this kind of spatial planning and development.

In developing a resource-rich region like this, there is always a danger of resorting to "extractive strategies", which will lead to leakage of natural resources from this region. The kind of turbulence and frustrations, which this region has already faced could be considerably exacerbated by such an indiscriminate approach. In this context, I would advocate a more cautious "*limited spatial closure strategy*", recommended by regional planners as the most suitable development option for this region at this point of time. This would imply a "stages approach" to development which, while protecting "the identity of this region" , would at the same time, give a chance for the region to develop the secondary lines of production in the region itself and thus augmenting the regional income through value addition.

Before I conclude my speech, I must emphasize another important point. This refers to the establishment of appropriate institutional mechanism and their close networking with other similar institutions in the country. One of the fortuitous development that has taken place in our country during the last two decades or so, is the emergence of quite a few non-governmental, policy-oriented research and development institutions in different parts, each with its own specialization in specific aspects of development planning. These institutions are throwing up valuable studies and ideas, which are influencing and shaping our development policies. It would be most ideal, if institutions with similar development objectives can network their operations and interact among themselves and thus pool their resources, both financial and personnel for their mutual benefit. It would pave the way not only for cost-effective research, but also enrich the quality of their contributions and above all to greater and quicker realization of their potentials. Further, I must add that in this matter of institutional networking, the simple mathematical law that 1 + 1 is equal to 2 is a fallacy. Here the summation is 11 and not 2. In other words, the whole is greater than the sum of its parts. The Institute of Interdisciplinary Studies that you have set up in this extreme corner of our country cannot stand alone. It should benefit through intensive interaction and dialogue with other institutions, located in different parts of the country and wedded to similar objectives. One organisation, which I can name to aid and assist you in this effort would be the Bhoovigyan Vikas Foundation, which was launched in April last year in New Delhi and which is fast developing as a Centre for Earth-Care Policy Studies. Besides its "think-tank" functions, it is also promoting "Museums of Earth, Man and Environment" in different parts of the country to spread the message of sustainable development. Perhaps, I cannot think of a better region for such a museum than the North-East, with its rich diversity of flora, fauna and indigenous cultures.

Friends, as you are embarking on this monumental task of engineering environmental management through Regional planning, let us remind ourselves of the words of Barbara Ward, one of those pioneers, who raised her lone voice of concern for 'Saving our Planet' in the sixties, by asserting that we should proceed in our task with "headstrong optimism and profoundly convinced that we shall overcome all obstacles".

I wish your deliberations in this conference all success and thank you for your kind indulgence and patience.

5

Transforming Village Clusters into Territorial Production Complexes

I. Introduction

In order to conceive a well-balanced model of rural development, economically, socially and environmentally, the Government of India hopes to evolve an Action Plan for making the Tenth Plan, a *People's Plan* and Development, a *People's Movement*. The programme announced for attaining this objective is through the establishment of *Knowledge Powered Village Complexes*, known by the acronym "*PURA*". (Provision of Urban amenities in Rural Areas) This is a key element of "Vision 2020" and is intended to give a new thrust to the all-round development of *viable village complexes* through the twin strategies of '*Effective Planning and Implementation of Rural Development Programmes with People's Participation*' and '*Effective Development Communication for People's Participation*'. The programme PURA is essentially a *Habitat Design* to achieve prosperous, peaceful and safe human habitat in rural areas that would improve the quality of life in rural places and lead to "*Inclusive Rural Development*".

The objective of this paper is to set the PURA Concept in the wider context of Holistic Village Cluster Development Planning to

* Address delivered in the M.S. Swaminathan Research Foundation at Chennai on 17-01-2004.

achieve "*Inclusive Development*". Given the initial push for the vision by the President of India, what is needed today is nothing less than spearheading a nation wide *Village Renewal Movement*, based on a wider understanding of the PURA concept.

II. The Concept of a Micro Territorial Production Complex

Our past experience has shown that conventional development strategies, which emphasize the growth of gross national product *per se*, without at the same time looking into area and community specific potentials and needs cannot alleviate mass poverty and unemployment. It is in this context that we advocate layered models of territorial production complexes in our rural areas to trigger off the full utilisation of natural resources and human potentials.

A Micro Level Rural Territorial Production Complex is a model of spatial organisation, envisaged as contributory to developing agriculture and allied activities as well as small and medium enterprises, effectively in the rural areas and to promote the welfare of rural residents. Ideally, such a Micro Level Territorial Production Complex should lead to rapid agricultural development in the villages and also produce and supply various equipments, materials and consumption goods necessary, with appropriate technology for a basic needs strategy, guiding the local development. It will provide the necessary backward and forward linkages and seek to augment the value addition to the agricultural products emerging from the rural areas and thus enrich the income of the local population. It is the linkages and flows, as well as the managerial improvements brought about to aid and facilitate the production activity in the primary villages, through encouragement and management of the production, processing and marketing activities in the functional area of a village cluster, that constitute the hallmarks of the concept of a Micro Rural Territorial Production Complex.

In such an approach, all incentive and subsidy programmes of the Government, as well as management, extension and training activities will be pooled and administered in a concerted manner to assist private initiatives in local areas. It will lead to a territorial division of labour, leading in due course to effective production relationships, determining the spatial structure of the economy at micro and mezo levels.

The strategy implied here must concentrate, more than in the past, on meeting the requirements of the small farmer, the small entrepreneur and the informal sector producer of services. Such a strategy calls for, and is in turn supported by, a special kind of appropriate technology, which will contain a greater element of technological innovation, governed by selective choice and adaptation applied to existing technologies.

In the context of our rural areas, the Micro Territorial Production Complex, as envisaged here, will be a relatively *Homogenous Community of Interest Area,* i.e. a *Village Cluster.*

III. Why A Village Cluster?

In our present development context, the Indian village, with its small population, has ceased to be an economic and social entity for planning. The knowledge century demands a size suitable for the effective transfer of technology. Besides, people would want higher forms of services and of quality in provisions like health, education, agricultural inputs and services etc. There is therefore, a need to think in terms of '*viable unit areas of development in rural space*'. It is in this context that the concept of a 'cluster of villages' comes as a useful grassroots level unit for planning, for organizing rural development programmes. It is not a new idea and has been discussed, since the middle of the 1960's, though no concerted efforts were made to operationalize the approach. Now, with the PURA concept gaining ground, there has been a revival of interest on this approach to micro-level planning.

IV. Evolution of the Concept

A review of the evolution of the thinking on 'village cluster approach' and of its relevance and usefulness as a tool for rural development would be a useful beginning to this discussion.

An early recognition of the concept was, when the First Master Plan for Delhi was prepared under the guidance of Albert Mayer of Etawah community development fame. The Delhi Master Plan adopted a hierarchical pattern of central villages, service centres and rural towns (based on Christaller's concept), for the limited purpose of bridging the rural-urban gap in the provision of social services[1]. A more concrete beginning towards this approach commenced when the Ford Foundation initiated in 1969, a *Pilot Research Project on Growth Centres* in collaboration with Govt. of India, envisaging a 'village cluster', around an identified growth centre, as an intermediate areal unit between the village and the block. It followed the typical spatial-cum-regional planner's approach of identifying a hierarchy of service centres (based on techniques like scalogram analysis), for extending a broad range of amenities, services and infrastructure to all settlements in the block. Thereafter, the sectoral scenarios of development are developed for agriculture, industry, education, health and transport to create an integrated spatial plan of development. This approach was also recommended by the Working Group on Block Level Planning, set up by the Planning Commission in 1978.[2]

Around the same time, an International Organization—The United Nations Research Institute for Social Development (UNRISD), Geneva, initiated research studies to examine the relevance of 'Growth Poles and Growth Centres' for regional development in the developing countries. We (Prof. R.P. Misra and myself) undertook a prestigious project funded by this organization to test the relevance of this concept in a most underdeveloped area of India. This led to our field study in 1963 in the Bastar district of Madhya Pradesh, a most backward tribal district. After this experience, we returned with rich insights and boldly stated our conviction that what are required to stimulate developments in such areas are "*Social Development Poles*", and '*People Centred Development*', rather than 'Growth Poles'. We viewed with great skeptism, the nature of '*modern*' developments taking place in the area by external agencies, e.g. the Bailadilla iron ore mining-developments, which were sweeping the economy of the tribals, '*off their feet*'.[3]

From the above experience stems our criticism about the mechanistic methodology, promoted through the spatial-cum-sectoral strategy, advocated by the growth pole researchers which, while using sophisticated criteria for determining the status of settlement centres (e.g. 'Population Threshold', Distance Norms', and Movement of People and Commodities'), blatantly ignored the inter and intra community relations in lower and grassroot level settlements and insights derived from the perception of rural contrasts and uneven economic and social development.

Since the 70's, the concept of rural development has undergone many changes. It is now "*Inclusive Socio-economic Development*", which inheres in it, the tasks of 'poverty reduction', 'employment generation', 'empowerment', 'equity', 'sustainable development of the natural resources', besides the provision of basic minimum services. It has *to be generated from "within"*, by unleashing the "*Capillary Mechanisms*" in the village situation, with people deciding their course of development and government supporting it. In this conception, the core tasks of rural development will include the fuller use of land and water resources without destruction, modernization of farming by extending processing and marketing activities, building non-farm and allied agricultural activities, setting up institutions like cooperatives and other forms of social capital, empowering panchayats and women and improving health and education services. We, therefore argue, that in order to bring about '*Inclusive Rural Development, with people's participation nexus*', the growth impulses need to be structured and built up at the level of "clusters of villages", in a highly integrated and effective manner. This line of reasoning implies a new perspective and a much deeper '*economic and social content*', of development addressed to both policy delivery and receiving sides. It is much more than ensuring merely a viable size of settlement for supporting a particular amenity or service. In this conception, the effectiveness of a 'cluster' at grassroot level depends not so much on the size alone of the population brought together, but on the degree of cohesiveness and integration among the constituent villages and social groups, quality of local leadership and capacity of rural institutions to bring the rural weak and poor within their fold. It is here that understanding the village as a part of rural neighbourhood assumes importance in planning for development. This new concept of rural development can be translated into action only through 'social animators' (committed NGO's) and 'change agents' (researchers) joining hands with local bureaucracy/technocracy and local people and their institutions. It has to be seen as a *joint endeavour* of various "*Partners in Progress*", with clear goals. (*Fig. 5.*)

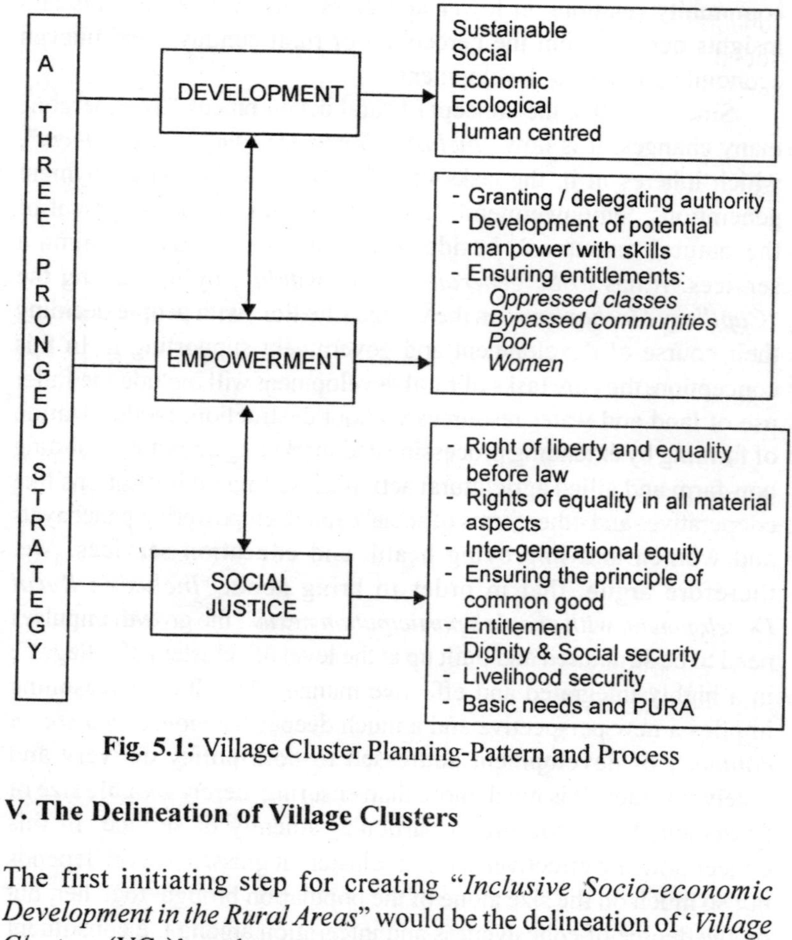

Fig. 5.1: Village Cluster Planning-Pattern and Process

V. The Delineation of Village Clusters

The first initiating step for creating "*Inclusive Socio-economic Development in the Rural Areas*" would be the delineation of '*Village Clusters* (VCs)' as the grassroot level units for rural planning and development. The ideal rural planning units would be the "*Cohesive Rural Community*", which can be delineated by taking into account the social, economic and spatial inter-relationships, as well as the power structure of the community. The Village Clusters (VCs) are thus envisaged as '*Community of Interest Areas* (CIAs)', in which people's association and social contacts will be of a voluntary nature, with people being drawn together by common interests in economic affairs, trade, social interests for recreation or religion etc. The focal point for each 'Community of Interest Area (CIAs)' will be a '*central place*' of viable population size, already performing some area-wide functions such as, school services, medical services, retail services, social and recreational services, business services and transport services. In order to delineate the hinterland of the selected central place, the analysis could proceed both from quantitative data available from secondary sources (e.g. for education and medical services), and combining this with enquiries made in the surrounding villages, so as to obtain a correct knowledge of those rural settlements, which customarily obtained a particular service from the given central place. Such investigations, coupled with the local knowledge of the relative "*pulls*" of the central places and the transport orientation and consumer travel patterns, will help to determine the hinterland of the selected central places. Mapping of "*Desire Lines*" for selected services in the rural areas may also be useful. With such methods, decisions about the central places and their hinterlands could be taken with a reasonable degree of accuracy.

Some of the studies made in micro-level planning in our country have concluded that a viable Village Cluster, which .would be the lowest area level unit for planning and development, may cover 5-6 contiguous villages, having a distance span of 4-6 kms and with a total population of about 8,000-10,000. One of our important Committees on Panchayati Raj, which studied the optimum size of the rural unit for planning and development has also concluded that "a large size of rural unit should be appropriate for the villager's own interest for input supplies and provision of services like hospitals and schools, warehousing facilities, availability of higher order technical services and a host of other inter-related functions, which forms part of the design of rural life" (Asok Mehta Committee, 1978).[4]

VI. PURA in its Wider Context

The case for Village Clusters (VCs) as grassroots level units for planning and development has been made in the previous paragraphs. The VC is only a structural component of rural development. We may now consider as to how to make it a really '*functional unit*', surging with dynamism and activities. In the '*structural plan*' that has been unfolded with the '*central place*' as the '*hub*' or '*node*', and with the constituent villages as the different '*spokes*', dynamism has to be infused through various human activities. Here comes the PURA concept to our aid, as a tool to infuse the 'nodes', with various forms of 'connectivities', 'flows', and 'iterative interactions'.

'*Nodes*' are 'Nodal/Focal' points, which are endowed with a certain minimum threshold of population, infrastructure and services, and which have the potential to propel activities relevant to development and radiate development impulses to surrounding villages.

The four critical '*connectivities*' to induce development are: (i) *Physical Connectivity* or road and transport and power connectivity to bridge distances; (ii) *Electronic Connectivity* to increase communication through media and digital opportunities; (iii) *Knowledge Connectivity* through education and imparting of skills and extension services to provide information, technology, and increased understanding; and (iv) *Market Connectivity* to link rural products to markets. The inadequate presence of these connectivities have been seen as the "*major irritants*", or obstacles to development in our rural areas and their removal is considered vital for rural transformation.

Simply providing connectivities will not do. They should be rendered *dynamic* through '*flows*', which have to be consciously induced in four directions viz. vertical, downward, horizontal, and circular. The '*Vertical Flows*' will provide bottom-up connectivity to higher order centres of activity for processing of commodities produced in primary villages and information on local needs and preferences, area priorities, targets, local problems and constraints. The '*Downward or Top-down Flows*' will provide macro-micro linkages and information flows relating to policies, priorities, targets, guidelines, budgetary and technical support. '*Horizontal Flows*' will establish inter and intra community information flows and interactions. '*Circular Flows*' will enhance the recycling-ratio within the villages, adding income to the village and bringing about a circular movement of commodities from the primary villages to their processing centres and the return movement of finished products to consumer centres.

'*Interactions*' constitute the vital component of this dynamic system and is closely related to both electronic connectivity and knowledge connectivity. It involves (a) the interaction of the people's institutions with government's institutions; (b) the interaction of people, as individuals, with their own institutions, like the Village Panchayat and Community-Based Organizations (CBO's); and (c) people to people informal interactions through their social organizations.

Thus, the planning intervention envisaged as "*Cluster Development*" and sought to be operationalized here through the nodes, connectivities, flows, and interactions, in space will ensure participatory development and enable bridging the rural-urban gap, providing urban amenities in rural areas (PURA) and enhancing the quality of life and livelihood opportunities for the rural people.

VII. The Operating Vision, Tactics and Planning

"Where there is no vision, the people perish" is a well-known axiom. It is only with a clear *operating vision* of objectives, thrusts, tactics, and programmatic interventions that any Village Cluster (VC) can hope to meet its '*tryst with destiny*'. Initially such a vision will never be totally explicit. It is latent, as a community's attitude towards itself and its aspirations are not easily visible. With iterative interaction with different sections of the community, however, this can be discovered with some clarity. With the modern tools of analyses, the vision that is latent could be objectified.

Tactical Planning

The discussion on 'Nodes', 'Connectivities', 'Flows' and 'Interactions' presented in the foregoing paragraphs relate to the *rebuilding of fundamental community structures* for the *Holistic Village Cluster Development Planning* in a multilevel framework (Fig. 5.2). They provide a broad framework for tactical planning i.e. for developing the tactics required to shape the destiny of the village. Thus tactical planning will describe and rationally organize the practical actions required for socio-economic change in the rural areas. The major tactical areas representing the 'overarching tasks' to be accomplished include:

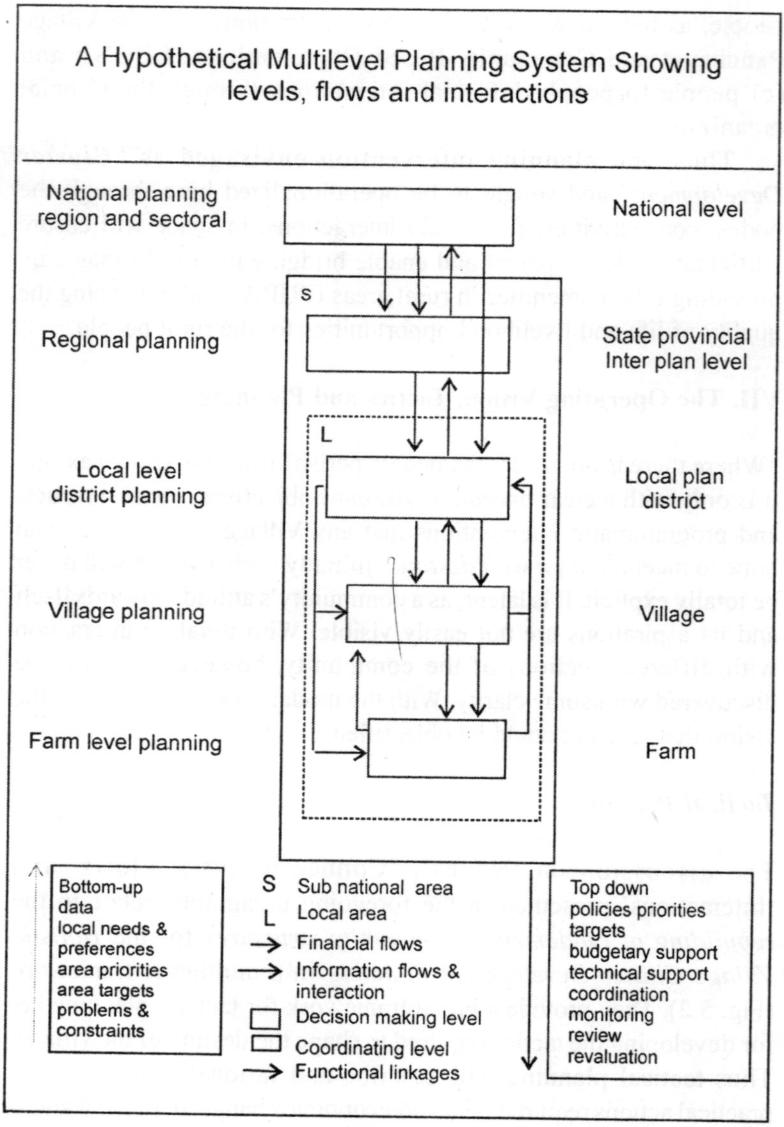

Fig. 5.2

(I) Creating an economically viable agricultural and industrial base for the village on the lines of an Auto-Kinetic Model of Development (Fig. 5.3). By auto-kinetic development, we

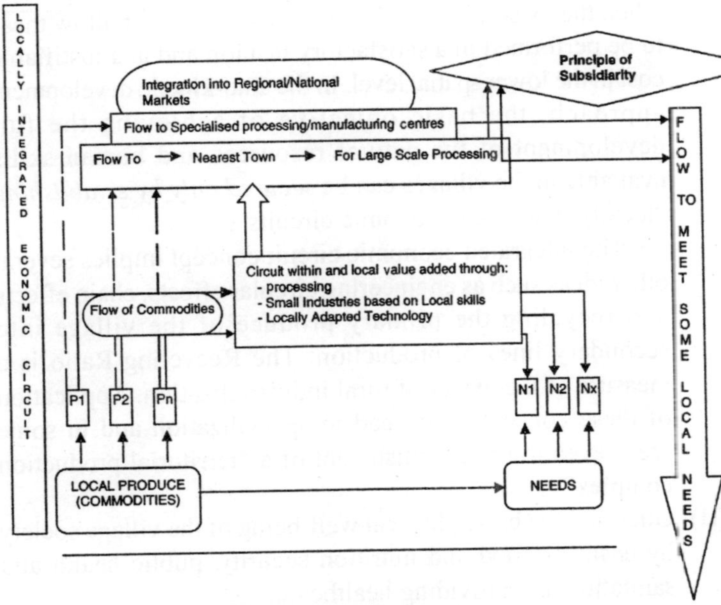

Fig. 5.3: Model of Auto-Kinetic

mean a process by which the auto-centric and auto-dynamic forcast of development can be unleashed, which will release the inner urges, potentials and energies inherent in the rural community. It is a process of engineering the overall development of productive forces, with the objective of better satisfying the basic livelihood and the material needs of the rural population, based as far as possible on a more intensive utilization of local resources, by means of locally adapted and locally controllable, labour-intensive and small-scale technologies. It is the same as the Gandhian concept of Village Swaraj or "Development from within", with the capillary mechanisms in place, but points to a definite method for augmenting rural incomes.

The auto-kinetic development process rests on the hierarchic principle of subsidiarity. That is, we seek to establish processing/manufacturing units at higher level, only when the existing technologies and skills do not allow these to be performed in a satisfactory fashion and at a justifiable cost in the lower spatial level. In the auto-kinetic development approach, the basic objective of achieving the full development of the natural resources and human skills available in the villages can be *secured only by establishing* "locally integrated economic circuits".

The integrated economic circuit concept implies several other ideas such as engineering circular effects, chain effects and recycling the primary produce of the village into secondary lines of production. The Recycling Ratio is a measure of the extent of rural industrialization. Application of these concepts may lead to specialization and in some areas even to the establishment of a "territorial production complex".

(II) Guarding the basic physical well-being of the village society by ensuring food and nutrition security, public health and sanitation and providing healthcare.

(III) Developing functional life skills, including upgrading of basic practical literacy skills at all age levels and providing practical training in marketable business and crafts and providing access to agricultural services including inputs and markets.

(IV) Another tactical arena would be breaking the isolation of the village and establishing external support relations. This could be established through fostering the necessary institutional relations with the Public and Private sectors and adapting the development programmes initiated by the government, to suit the local specificities and needs, forging extended business contacts, e.g. for securing bank loans to fund local projects and promoting the village public image.

(V) Leveraging Information and Communication Technology (ICT) is one of the major tactics for transforming the village into a knowledge-based society. This would call for establishing a "Knowledge Communication Centre (KCC)" *and training the rural youth in computer literacy. In this manner,* agricultural information for precision farming from extension agencies and price signals *from neighbouring market centres could be accessed by the rural community. The* 'Hub and Spoke Model' *for a knowledge communication centre is illustratively indicated in Fig. 5.4.* the planning framework for the arching dimensions of the operating vision may be visualized in five broad groups viz. community sustenance; habitat improvement; sustainable development; institutional support; and social awakening. Each group has been further elaborated to indicate the major thrusts and further detailed into 'enabling programmatic interventions', for actuating the 'Vision'. These are outlined in Table-1, which illustrates study in a nutshell.

Objectives (Broad Groups)	*Major Thrusts*	*Programmatic Interventions*
Community Sustenance (upgrading the economic foundations of village life)	1. Agri-Production Complex 2. Food and Nutrition Security 3. Full Employment	Production and productivity increase, Transportation, Marketing and credit Linkages, product diversification Grain Golas; and Effective PDS; Livestock/Poultry/Horticulture development SME's through Integrated Economic Circuit
Habitat Improvement	4. Village Reconstruction and provision of basic amenities	Housing rehabilitation, Public utilities and facilities, Power, communication and transport systems
Sustainable Development	5. Ecodevelopment (Biovillage)-Promoting conservation and job-led growth opportunities.	Land and Water Management; bio-diversity conservation
Institutional Support	6. Poly-centric Planning and Management Institutions	Village Planning Forum, Village Skill Development Centre, Village Knowledge and Communication Centre Cooperatives, User Groups, And CBO's.
Social Awakening	7. Social Rebuilding (Through social animators)	Training and education for social effectivity, Literacy training, Training for women/youth, Land Army, Barefoot Doctors/Engineers/Technologists etc.

Fig. 5.4: Holistic Village Cluster Development Project *Operating Vision*

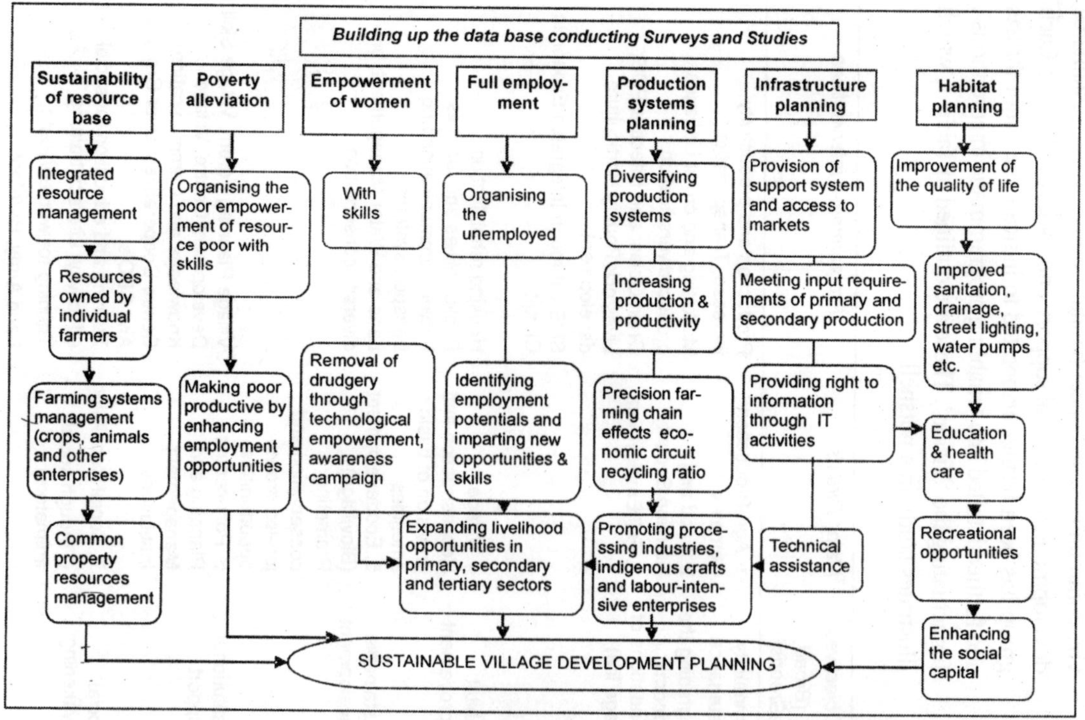

Fig. 5.5: Holistic Planning for a Village Cluster Concepts and Key Dimensions

Programme Content

Successful implementation of the Holistic Village Cluster Development strategy requires complex decentralized matrix structures, with permanent mechanisms for vertical and lateral integration, a combination of specialist and generalist skills, institutional leadership, social intervention capability and systems management. The methodology and programme content would include the building up of the databases for decision-making through secondary and primary surveys and selected studies conducted by using PURA methods. A seven-fold programmatic design is advocated which will aim at (1) Ensuring Sustainability of Resource Base, (ii) Poverty Alleviation, (iii) Empowerment of Women, (iv) Full Employment, (v) Production Systems Planning, (vi) Infrastructure Planning and (vii) Habitat Planning. These are further elaborated in the accompanying Flow Chart (*Fig. 5.5*). The Bhoovigyan Vikas Foundation hopes to seek to translate the operating vision elucidated in this paper into a few pilot projects in different typological areas.

The operating vision for rural development outlined in this paper and many of its underlying concepts bear a close imprint of Mahatma Gandhi's vision for the reclaiming of the rural villages across our country.

VI. Expected Outputs

There will be the following major outputs from this project.

1. It will establish a methodology for "Micropolitan-centred Village Cluster Development" in a participatory-cum-research action mode, with the Panchayati Raj Institutions, Village Leaders, Community-based Organisations, NGO's and a Team of Researchers joining hands in a common endeavour of village development through social mobilization.
2. It will initiate a village development movement in the country through auto-kinetic processes aimed at a pro-nature, pro-poor, pro-employment and pro-women development paradigm of sustainable agriculture and rural development.

3. The project will enable a critical mass of village youth to be trained in planning and implementation of rural development activities.
4. It will enable the Ministry of Rural Development, Government of India to issue appropriate Guidelines on Village Development Planning to the State Governments.

This exercise will be a valuable input to the formulation of village action programmes during the 10th Five Year Plan in respect of operationalising micro-level planning at the grassroots level, all over the country through the Panchayati Raj Institutions and other "partners in progress" and initiating a "Rural Renaissance Movement" in the country.

IX. The Project Sites

The project is proposed to be undertaken in all the five ecosystems of the country, viz. one district each in Hilly ecosystem, Coastal ecosystem, Rainfed ecosystem, Irrigated ecosystem, and Arid ecosystem.

REFERENCES

1. Sundaram, K.V. 'Service Centres and community of interest Areas: A Case Study of Rural Delhi' in *Urban and Regional Planning In India*, Vikas Publishing House, New Delhi, 1977. Reprinted in 'The Trodden Path—Essays in Regional and Micro-level Planning, Anamaya Publishers, New Delhi, 2004.
2. *Report of the Working Group on Block Level Planning*, Government of India, Planning Commission, 1978.
3. Sundaram, K.V. "Spatial Planning for a Tribal Region" in *Urban and Regional Planning in India,* Vikas Publishing House, New Delhi, 1977.
4. *Report of the Committee on Panchayati Raj Institutions*, Government of India, Ministry of Agriculture and Irrigation, New Delhi, August 1978.
5. Misra, R.P., Sundaram, K.V. and Rao, V.L.S. Prakasa, "Regional *Development Planning in India : A New Strategy*", Vikas Publishing House, New Delhi, 1977.
6. Sundaram, K.V. "*Decentralized Multilevel Planning : Principles and Practice (Asian and African Experiences)*", Concept Publishing Company Pvt. Ltd, New Delhi, 1997.

III
Land Use Policy

6

Sustainable Land Use Policy: Contextualities and Capabilities

We are now living in the worst of times in human history, with the repeated bludgeonings of Nature's fury taking its full revenge on Man's greedy deeds on 'Earth'. Having, experienced the worst of natural disasters—tsunami, floods, drought and earthquakes—during the last two years, we are now deeply aware that this Earth, our home, is in a great crisis. I recall how in the 1960's and 70s, the well-known British environmental activist and ardent advocate of Earth Care Campaign, Mrs. Barbara Ward used to emphasize in her lectures, marked by great oratorical skills, that '*Saving this one and only Earth*', the one only the living planet in our solar system, should be an important item in the development agenda of the developing and developed nations today. She warned that the time is not quite far-off before the planet suffers the full consequences of acid rain, global warming, ozone depletion, widespread desertification and species loss. Ultimately, her vigorous advocacy led to the U.N., taking note of the Earth's crisis, setting up the World Commission on Environment and Development, headed by Mrs. Brundtland, whose report on '*Our Common Future*' is well known. This report emphasised that 'THERE IS NOT MUCH TIME LEFT FOR OUR PLANET TO BE SAVED'.

---

* Key Note Address delivered in the National Conference on 'Land Use and Land Cover Management Practices' held on 21/22 August, 2005 at Hyderabad, organized by the Centre for Land Use Management, Hyderabad.

1. The sweeping socio-economic developments in the world have resulted in many problems that are endangering not only the present and the future generations on this earth, but also the equality and equity aspects of development among nations and peoples. What we now need are proper policies put in place, to guide our planning and development issues. Appropriate land use policy is one of these formulations. That defines our problem and its urgency today.

2. The Eight 'Avatars' (Manifestations) of Growth

The last century has bequeathed us many difficult problems. We sought '*Growth*', as the ultimate goal. It was a mania with the planners, and as a result, many '*ugly*' forms of growth have appeared on the scene. I can count at least eight of them, which have characterised our fifty years of Development Struggle.

(i) *Jobless growth* i.e. Growth without employment opportunities
(ii) *Ruthless growth* i.e. Growth that has aggravated the inequalities
(iii) *Futureless growth* i.e. Growth that has inhibited the development of future generations
(iv) *Voiceless growth* i.e. Non-participatory growth or growth that has deprived the participation of by-passed groups in society.
(v) *Rootless growth* i.e. Growth that has destroyed the cultural roots of our society
(vi) *Inequitable growth* i.e. Growth without redistribution
(vii) *Unsustainable growth* i.e. Growth which has been environmentally destructive.
(viii) *Dependent growth* i.e. Growth without self-reliance.

3. In this new century, we are now facing all the '*dilemmas*' of this ugly growth. What are the prospects before us? Alvin Tofler in his book on "*The Third Wave*", had envisioned a '*global village*', which has now become a reality. Now geographical boundaries have little meaning and we have an "*International trade regime*", organised by the World Trade Organisation—with free trade and investment as its principal tenets—that is dictating our path to development. But it is being sought to be so framed as to favour the Developed Countries, threatening the socio-cultural fabrics of our traditional agriculture, leaving the nearly half of the population of the developing world, who are small farmers, on the verge of being marginalized. Thus with many people rendered '*living on the edge*' of a futureless precipice, we are now on the throes of defining policies for the sustainable management of our land resources.

4. Contextuality and Capability

With these preliminary observations, I now come to the mainstream of our discussion on "'Sustainable Development and Management of our Land Resources". To begin with, I would like to clear some conceptual cobwebs. The term 'Land Use' is *not* to be understood, merely in the sense of an allocation process—i.e. allocation of land for different uses—but must be seen in a wider context of "*Inclusive Development*", whose bottom-line is defined by economics, ecology and equity. Since it is Man, who is putting the land and its biotic resources to their different 'uses', it has to be seen in the context of the interface of "*Earth and Man*".

5. The Nobel laurette Amartya Sen[1] has convincingly argued in many of his writings that the goal of development is to expand people's '*capability*' to do things that they have a reason to cherish and value. His '*Capability Approach*' enunciates a theory of '*value*' and '*ethic*' for assessing possibility and achievability. His ideas related to '*capability*' has been widely applied in planning in different contexts.[1] I have sought to apply it to Land Use Planning.

You will all agree that any assessment of land and its different uses for various purposes must recognize the constraints and opportunities for development. Land use, as determined by scientists, is usually based on a rigorous assessment and mapping of physical (Geomorphological, Soil and Ecological) attributes using satellite imagery and ground, truthing methods. It does not take note of the

1. Sen, A.K. (1990b) "*Development as a capability expansion*" in Griffin K. Knight J. (Eds.), *Human Development and the International Development strategy for the 1990's* (Macmillan in association with the United Nations: London), pp. 41-58.

constraints, which are individual or "*farmer-based preferences*", such as culture, traditional knowledge systems, community values and social dynamics. Thus one is a scientific decision-making level and the other is at the '*People level*'. In the way that land use planning is practiced by scientists, there is a relative neglect of the people-level processes in decision-making. In other words, for establishing a conceptual framework for assessing the determinants of Land Use Policies, a conscious blend of the core ideas related to '*capability at people level*', with an understanding of the potentials and constraints, emerging from a scientific analysis of Geographic or Space perspective is not taking place. This blend i.e. '*Earth-Man-Space nexus*' is the concept of '*socio-spatial milieu*' i.e. space fashioned by human action. It is *Relational or Contextual Space* in which people have developed their unique institutional formations relating to social, cultural, economic and political arrangements.

6. It refers not only to the visible elements of Geographic space i.e. physical features, landforms and natural resource elements, but also to the relatively non-visible human values i.e. social relations, culture, hopes and aspirations of the local community. It is space fashioned by human action. According to a French philosopher, Vidal de la Blache, this space is like "*a medal struck in the likeness of the people*", referring to the anthropogenic influences on the lithosphere.

7. This concept of Relational or Contextual Space makes a lot of difference in our developmental thinking process. In the works on land use planning done by many agricultural scientists, and soil scientists, I find that the land use prescriptions are mainly determined by the physical attributes, especially climate, topography and soils, as the term '*land capability*' used in this context very clearly indicates. Studies conducted by social scientists in different parts of the world have, however, tended to discredit this approach as '*oversimplistic*' and observed that environmentally similar areas have been developed in quite dissimilar ways by their inhabitants. This means that the human attributes of an area, which include social structures, cropping patterns, ways of life and even the traditions, culture, habits and temperament of the inhabitants, play a crucial role in the determination of land use. These attributes constitute, what I would call the "*Human ecosystems*", approach. A concept which implies the notion that individuals and groups relate to their environments through their perception or cognition of them. Among the drivers of Land Use/ Land Cover change[2], the most important are the human beings and this underlines the importance of inscribing human values into our Land Use analysis.

8. Bridging Determinism and Possibilism—Towards an Adaptive Approach

If we accept this concept of "*human ecosystems approach*", then land use must be seen in the context of "*improving our rural livelihoods*", in accordance with human capabilities, traditional knowledge and cultural traits. That would make all the differences in our methodology of land use planning. It would mean bringing in the concept of an "*Adaptive Approach*", which is quite different from the "*deterministic land capability approach*" of physical scientists.

9. The term Land capability as defined by physical scientists, implies "*optimality*" with reference to physical attributes only. It is a tight-jacketed '*Territorial Control*' of land use. On the other hand, the adaptive approach i.e. linking people with resources implies a flexible, workable and balanced approach, weighing various human capabilities and possibilities. It underlines the concept of "*possibilism*". This difference between "*determinism*" and "*possibilism*" must be carefully understood. Let me quote again the famous French geographer Vidal de La Blache, who said "*There are no necessities, but everywhere, possibilities, and Man as the master of these possibilities is the best judge of their use*". In my view, the 'Adaptive Approach', which I am advocating, will bridge the deterministic and possibilistic schools of thought and would be quite relevant to our times. The 'Adaptive approach' also implies the integration of the good features in our traditional land use methods with the modern scientific methods.

---

2. The various factors driving Land Use/Land Cover changes acting at local, regional and global levels are: (i) Population growth, change in population structure and migration, (ii) Demands for energy, products and amenities (consumption patterns, tourism), (iii) Lifestyle and rural-urban interactions, (iv) Extreme events and variability in biophysical conditions, (v) Macro–economic drivers, (vi) National Policy measures and directives, (vii) External drivers (Globalisation, trade regimes, international agreements)

10. Land Use Planning: Challenges and Tasks

Now let me briefly outline the challenges and tasks in Land Use Planning. It is the maladjustment between human society and its environments which is the greatest problem that we will be facing in the new millennium. This "Maladjustment", is caused by both human factors, such as land degradation, droughts or famines and their whole nexus of related problems. Preventing this disaster and restoring eroded and damaged lands through appropriate land use policies and strategies is a scientific and technical challenge of the first order.

11. This millennium

It presupposes the optimization of the following tasks:

(i) Massive increase in agricultural production both in the medium and long term to safeguard a sufficient supply of food for the growing population, that we will have at the end of this millennium.
(ii) The repairing of ecological damage to be tackled at the same time to enable transition to an *ecologically adapted land use.*
(iii) The need for environmentally acceptable ways of thinking, acting and addressing the issues in agricultural development, not merely from a national and regional perspective, but also from an *intensely local perspective*, taking note of Global imperatives.
(iv) Blending the best of modern science with traditional wisdom and the ecological prudence of local societies.

The implementation of the above tasks requires not merely the application of a great deal of science and technology, but also a very high measure of moral/humanitarian solidarity and participatory effort among the rural folk, who are the real stakeholders. All these tasks call for an effort to meet the challenges of a shift to the paradigm of sustainable development.

12. What does this Paradigm Shift mean?

It means essentially, a shift to ecologically-oriented ways of thinking and patterns of action. Such action should proceed not merely from a local or regional perspective. It means a progressive condensation, as well as integration of time and space and increasing man's tightening bondage to the environment, by operationalising a plan for "working with Nature". Such development transition would call for new and future-oriented concepts firstly in precision farming for enhanced productivity and secondly in land use change for diversification of livelihood opportunities.

13. The New Imperatives

Let us now take stock of our new imperatives in agricultural land use planning. The Green Revolution (GR) during 1970's and 1980's, led to the achievement of near self-sufficiency in food production. This was no doubt a distinct gain. Now the Green Revolution is facing a new set of challenges posed by the excessive use of chemical fertilizers and pesticides. It has to be rendered *evergreen* as emphasised by Dr. M.S. Swaminathan. We are also faced with an imperative to relate our developments to the external factors of globalization, liberalization and privatisation of the production and trade regime. Our priorities today are the need to bring about necessary changes in our policies to negotiate these problems, to enhance production, and to increase the opportunity and productivity for off-farm employment and value addition through agro-processing and other Small and Medium Enterprises (SME's). The major challenge before us is: how to maintain and enhance the integrity of the natural resource base, while at the same time increasing productivity and value addition.

14. Bertrand Russel once said. "One must look into *hell* before one has any right to speak of *heaven*". When applied in the context of achieving sustainable development, this means that we must first examine and correct the 'ecological footprints' left by Man, before building up any model of sustainable development. If that is so, our topmost priority is to take the corrective steps for checking land degradation and accelerating efforts towards ecological restoration.

15. Spreading a Land Care Movement

This would call for spreading a *Land Care Movement,* inscribing some elements of "*Returning to Nature*" and adopting some good features inherent in our traditional forms of land use and soil management. The next decade is a decade for "*Agricultural Land Use Renaissance*". Our national land use and land management policies should address these issues. If the Land Care Movement is to be effectively organised in a vast country like ours, we need to build up an effective "*Land Army*" in each village, by organising local youth as *social activists*. They will actively interface with agricultural scientists and disseminate knowledge on restoring our degraded lands and enhancing their productivity. I recall that one retired Brigadier in the state of Karnataka in the 1960's initiated a Land Care Movement in that State and also wrote a book on "*Land Army*". As a lone person advocating this idea, he could not do much at that time, when the development organisational set-up in the country was weak and extension services were hardly available. Today, with a better organisational set-up, it is perhaps worth giving a push to this idea of "*Local Land Army*" in each village to promote land conservation. I also recall that the same idea was articulated by Dr. Akhtar Hameed Khan, a distinguished administrator turned social scientist in the 1950's, who advocated the "Comilla Approach to Rural Development" in Bangladesh.

16. Multi-level Land Use Policies

Land Use Policy at the National level should effectively respond to the global imperatives of sustainable development, within the free market paradigm. It should address itself to six axioms:

(i) Reviving a reasonably sustainable growth;
(ii) Changing the quality of growth;
(iii) Meeting essential need for jobs, energy, water and sanitation;
(iv) Conserving and enhancing the resource base;
(v) Reorienting technology and managing risk; and
(vi) Integrating environment and economics in decision making;

Our Land Use Policy at the National level should also seek to address issues such as the role of Biotechnology, Agricultural Technologies in different Eco-systems, Bio-diversity and Institutional

Reforms. It should also draw up a broad policy framework in the context of globalisation, liberalisation and other external influences. At the intermediate or regional (State) level, it is a task of Regional Agricultural Land Use Planning, seeking to optimize uses, spelling out the right allocation of land, the right management of land and a fair distribution of its products.

17. Regional Land Use Planning

At the regional (State) level, Land use planning will have to be in the nature of "*Economic-cum-Environmental (EcE) planning*", interweaving economic, natural resources, environmental and human resource development planning. For this, the State must be sub-divided into relatively homogenous regions on agro-climatic-ecological basis[3]. For each sub-region, the overall development strategies should be formulated within an agreed set of guiding principles and an "*Economic-cum-Environmental Action Plan*" should be drawn up. A rigorous eco-management action plan would involve assessing the maximum utility value of sub-regional land resources by valuation models involving multi-objective linear programming, multi-criteria analysis and trade-off analysis. For accomplishing this, the Land Use Boards must be equipped with professionals with multi-disciplinary training. They should use Geographical Information Systems approach based on satellite derived data coupled with ground truth verification. The Bhoovigyan Vikas Foundation has prepared the training modules for this purpose. It can share this with the Land Use Planning Boards for jointly holding training programmes.

18. Micro Level Land Use Planning

19. Now let me touch on land use planning at *Micro level,* to which I attach great importance. At the micro level, land use planning will be a community-based and farm-based approach, using Participatory Rural Appraisal (PRA) methods. Prof. Swaminathan,

---

3. The Planning Commission has identified 15 agro-climatic zones and 73 sub-zones for Agro-Climatic Resource Planning. Adopting Human Ecosystems approach, several typologies of socio-economic regions could also be identified.

who innovated the "*Green Revolution*", has advocated the 'Bio-village model' of rural development, with its thrust on "pro-poor, pro-job and pro-women approach' He calls it the "Evergreen Revolution", which will bring about radical transformation in the countryside. The Bhoovigyan Vikas Foundation has further stretched this model to incorporate production, processing and marketing systems into an interlinked *auto-kinetic development process*, with its hierarchic principle of '*subsidiarity*' and the establishment of '*integrated economic circuits*', involving circular flows, chain effects and recycling ratios. It is a holistic Village Cluster Approach, incorporating the principles of the PURA Concept. It can be operationalised through a massive *Land Care Movement* for bringing about '*Rural Renaissance*'. In order to move towards such Rural Renaissance and operationalise participatory planning, the Land Use Boards must network with a number of local NGOs.

20. The Bhoovigyan Vikas Foundation has prepared a project proposal for "*Village cluster development planning*", which while retaining the basic principles of eco-development, emphasizes the promotion of increased avenues for rural non-farm employment. This will stem from an 'auto-kinetic model' of development, for better satisfying the basic livelihood and the material needs of the rural population, through appropriate technologies.

The micro level planning, as envisaged here, should emerge from a "*Technocratic-Academic-Democratic Mix (TAD Mix) Approach*", adopted in the model of Kundrakudi development in Tamil Nadu. It will be a partnership approach in research-cum-action mode, involving the technocrats in government, the academic community and professional NGO's working in tandem with local Panchayats and community-based organisations.

21. Towards Convergence and Synergy: Role of Land Use Boards It is obvious that given the range of land use policy measures that need to be implemented at the different levels—national, regional and local—and the cooperative effort needed on the part of various agents—namely the government, community based organisations and the many individual decision-takers, constituting the large private sector—only a '*synergestic approach*' can bring about an "*Agricultural Land Use Renaissance,*" which the new millennium calls for. To facilitate such renaissance, Dr. Swaminathan has advocated a *National Land Use Advisory Service*, operated through State Land Use Boards, which will disseminate agricultural information relating to ecological, meteorological and marketing factors, on a location and season-specific basis. This should be linked to *State, Block and Village Level Land Use Advisory Services*, which will greatly assist farmers in pro-actively organising their activities for precision farming. The core elements of this organisational structure are already there. They need to be strengthened and suitably revitalised. In this way, the Land Use Boards can serve as "*Inspirational Guideposts*" to farmers in the country.

The task of evolving a holistic and sustainable agricultural land use planning system in the country is challenging, but certainly not beyond the collective wisdom of our people and scientists. Where there is a will, there is a way. All it needs is a collective and united effort with commitment and dedication. In the mid-1930's, the land use land cover maps for the entire country of Great Britain were prepared using student power, through the motivation and commitment of a Professor of Geography in the University of London, Prof. Dudley Stamp. Those were days, when such refined tools like remote sensing and satellite imageries were not available. Now with the remarkable advances made in these directions, we can achieve much more, with devotion and commitment.

7

Sustainable Management of Land Resources: The Challenges before the Current Millennium

I am deeply impressed with the title of this National Seminar, which stresses the importance of the Land Care Movement. This is in congruence with the objectives of the Bhoovigyan Vikas Foundation, which I represent, and which advocates a nation-wide *Earth Care Movement,* which comprises not only the care of Lithosphere, but also those of the Hydrosphere, the Atmosphere and the Biosphere. Among these, Land Care is basic to harness our agro-bio-diversity and to realise the potential of our production systems on a sustained basis. In our present context of mounting demographic pressure and challenges related to sustainable enhanced agricultural production, it calls for vital changes and departures in our mindset including values, economics and community endeavour different from those that prevail today.

1. Having experienced the worst of natural disasters during the last year, we have become deeply aware that the Earth, our home, is now in a great crisis. "*Saving this one and only Earth*" as Barbara Ward, the well-known and revered British Eco-Economist often used to say, is an important item in our Development Agenda today. Many

---

* Key Note Address delivered in the National Seminar on 'Sustainable Management of Land Resources through Land Care Movement' held on 12-13 January, 2006 at Lucknow, organised by the State Land Use Board, Uttar Pradesh.

well-known scientists and visionaries have opined that "*There is not much time left for our planet to be saved*". The sweeping socio-economic developments in the world have resulted in many problems that are endangering not only the present and the future generations on this earth, but also equality and equity in development among nations and people, unless proper policies are put in place, to guide our planning. Land use policy is one of these formulations. That defines our problem and its urgency today.

The last century has bequeathed us many difficult problems. We sought "*Growth*", as the ultimate goal. It was a mania with the planners, and as a result, many '*ugly*' forms of growth have appeared on the scene. I can count at least eight of them, which have characterised our fifty years of Development Struggle.

2. The Eight 'Avatars' (Manifestations) of Growth

(i) Jobless growth i.e. Growth without employment opportunities.
(ii) Ruthless growth i.e. Growth that has aggravated the inequalities.
(iii) Futureless growth i.e. Growth that has inhibited the development of future generations.
(iv) Voiceless growth i.e. Non-participatory growth or growth that has deprived the participation of by-passed groups in society.
(v) Rootless growth i.e. Growth that has destroyed the cultural roots of our society.
(vi) Inequitable growth i.e. Growth without redistribution.
(vii) Unsustainable growth i.e. Growth which has been environmentally destructive.
(viii) Dependent growth i.e. Growth without self-reliance.

In this new century, we are now facing all the '*dilemmas*' of this ugly growth. What are the prospects before us? Alvin Tofler in his book on "*The Third Wave*", had envisioned a '*global village*', which has now become a reality. Now geographical boundaries have little meaning and we have an "*International trade regime*", organised by the World Trade Organisation—with free trade and investment as its principal tenets—that is dictating our path to development. But it is being sought to be so framed as to favour the Developed Countries, threatening the socio-cultural fabrics of our traditional agriculture, leaving the nearly half of the population of the developing world, who are small farmers, on the verge of being marginalized. Thus with many people rendered '*living on the edge*' of a futureless precipice, we are now on the throes of defining policies for the sustainable management of our land resources. I congratulate the organisers of this National Seminar for choosing a topic of considerable importance for lively exchange of views at this right time.

3. Land Use policies and the 'Human Ecosystems Approach'

With these preliminary observations, I now come to the mainstream of our discussion on 'Sustainable Management of Land Resources through appropriate Land Use Policies'. To begin with, I would like to clear some conceptual cobwebs. The term 'Land Use' is *not* to be understood, merely in the sense of an allocation process—i.e. allocation of land for different uses—but must be seen in a wider context of what is called "*Inclusive Development*", whose bottom-line is defined by economics, ecology and equity. Since it is Man, who is putting the land and its biotic resources to their different 'uses', it has to be seen in the context of the interface of "*Earth and Man*". This '*relational space*' or '*Contextual Space*', refers not only to the visible elements of Geographic space i.e. physical features, landforms and natural resource elements, but also to the relatively non-visible human values i.e. social relations, culture, hopes and aspirations of the local community. It is space fashioned by human action. According to a French philosopher, Vidal de la Blache, this space is like "*a medal struck in the likeness of the people*", referring to the anthropogenic influences on the lithosphere. This concept of Relational or Contextual Space makes a lot of difference in our developmental thinking process.

4. The Human Ecosystems Approach

In the works on land use planning done by many agricultural scientists, and soil scientists, I find that the land use prescriptions are mainly determined by the physical attributes, especially climate, topography and soils, as the term '*land capability*' used in this context very clearly indicates. Studies conducted by social scientists in different parts of the world have, however, tended to discredit this approach as 'oversimplistic' and observed that environmentally similar areas have been developed in quite dissimilar ways by their inhabitants. This means that the human attributes of an area, which include social structures, cropping patterns, ways of life and even the traditions, culture, habits and temperament of the inhabitants, play a crucial role in the determination of land use. These attributes constitute, what I would call the "*Human ecosystems*", approach—a concept which implies the notion that individuals and groups relate to their environments through their perception or cognition of them. This underlines the importance of inscribing human values into our 'Land use analysis'.

5. The Adaptation Approach: Bridging Determinism and Possiblism

If we accept this concept of "*human ecosystems approach*", then land use must be seen in the context of "*improving our rural livelihoods*", in accordance with human capabilities and cultural traits. That would make all the difference in our methodology of land use planning. It would mean bringing in the concept of an "*Adaptive Approach*", which is quite different from the "*deterministic land capability approach*" of physical scientists.

6. Land capability implies "*optimality*" with reference to physical attributes only. It is a tight-jacketed 'Territorial Control' of land use. On the other hand, the adaptive approach implies a flexible, workable and balanced approach, weighing various human capabilities and possibilities. It underlines the concept of "*possibilism*". This difference between "*determinism*" and "*possibilism*" must be carefully understood. Let me quote again the famous French philosopher Vidal de la Blache, who said "*There are no necessities, but everywhere, possibilities, and Man as the master of these possibilities is the best judge of their use*" In my view, the 'Adaptive Approach' which I am advocating will bridge the deterministic and possibilistic schools of thought and would be quite relevant to our times. The 'Adaptive approach' also implies the integration of the good features in our traditional land use methods with the modern scientific methods.

7. Challenges and Tasks in Land Use Planning

Now let me briefly outline the challenges and tasks in Land Use Planning. It is the maladjustment between human society and its environments which is the greatest problem that we will be facing in the new millennium. This "Maladjustment", is caused by both human and natural factors, such as land degradation, droughts or famines and their whole nexus of related problems. Preventing this disaster and restoring eroded and damaged lands through appropriate land use policies and strategies is a scientific and technical challenge of the first order.

8. It has to be seen in the context of 'Social Transformation' and presupposes the optimisation of the following tasks:

(i) A massive increase in agricultural production both in the medium and long term to safeguard a sufficient supply of food for the growing population, that we will have at the end of this millennium.
(ii) The repairing of ecological damage to be tackled at the same time to enable transition to an *ecologically adapted land use.*
(iii) The need for environmentally acceptable ways of thinking, acting and addressing the issues in agricultural development, not merely from a national and regional perspective, but also from an *intensely local perspective*, taking note of Global imperatives.
(iv) Blending the best of modern science with traditional wisdom and the ecological prudence of local societies.

The implementation of the above tasks requires not merely the application of a great deal of science and technology, but also a very high measure of moral/humanitarian solidarity and participatory effort among the rural folk, who are the real stakeholders. All these tasks call for an effort to meet the challenges of a shift to the paradigm of sustainable development.

9. What does this Paradigm Shift Mean?

It means essentially, a shift to ecologically-oriented ways of thinking and patterns of action. Such action should proceed not merely from a local or regional perspective. It means a progressive condensation, as well as integration of time and space and man's tightening bondage to the environment, by operationalising a plan for "*working with Nature*". Such development transition would call for new and future-oriented concepts firstly in precision farming for enhanced productivity and secondly in land use change for diversification of livelihood opportunities.

10. The New imperatives

Let us now take stock of our new imperatives in our agricultural land use planning.

The Green Revolution (GR) during 1970's and 1980's, led to the achievement of near self-sufficiency in food production. This was no doubt a distinct gain. Now the Green Revolution is facing a new set of challenges posed by the excessive use of chemical fertilizers and pesticides. It has to be rendered *evergreen*. We are also faced with an imperative to relate our developments to the external factors of globalization, liberalization and privatisation of the production and trade regime. Our priorities today are the need to bring about necessary changes to negotiate these problems, to enhance production and productivity, and to increase the opportunities for off-farm employment and value addition through agro-processing and other Small and Medium Enterprises.(SME's). The major challenge before us is how to maintain and enhance the integrity of the natural resource base, while at the same time increasing productivity and value addition.

11. Spreading a Land Care Movement

This would call for spreading a *Land Care Movement,* inscribing some elements of "*Returning to Nature*" and adopting some good features inherent in our traditional forms of land use and soil management. The next decade is a decade for "*Agricultural Land*

Use Renaissance". Our national land use and land management policies should address these issues. If the Land Care Movement is to be effectively organised in a vast country like ours, we need to build up an effective "*Land Army*" in each village, by organising local youth as social activists. This will actively interface with agricultural scientists and disseminate knowledge on restoring our degraded lands and enhancing their productivity. I recall that one retired Brigadier in the state of Karnataka in the 1960's initiated a Land Care Movement in that State and also wrote a book on "*Land Army*". As a lone person advocating this idea, he could not do much at that time, when the development organisational set-up in the country was weak and extension services were hardly available. Today, with a better organisational set-up, it is perhaps worth giving a push to this idea of "*Local Land volunteers,' Activists*" in each village to promote land conservation. I also recall that the same idea was articulated by Dr. Akhtar Hameed Khan, a distinguished Civil Administrator turned Social Scientist in the 1950's, who advocated the "*Comilla Approach to Rural Development*" in Bangladesh.

Multi-level Land Use Policies should be clearly formulated for different area levels.

12. Land Use Policy at Different Spatial Levels

Land use policy at the National level should effectively respond to the global imperatives of sustainable development, within the free market paradigm. It should address itself to six axioms:

1. Reviving a reasonably sustainable growth;
2. Changing the quality of growth;
3. Meeting essential need for jobs, energy, water and sanitation;
4. Conserving and enhancing the resource base;
5. Reorienting technology and managing risk; and
6. Integrating environment and economics in decision making.

Our Land Use Policy at the National level should also seek to address issues such as the role of Biotechnology, Agricultural Technologies in different Eco-systems, Bio-diversity and Institutional

Reforms. It should also draw up a broad policy framework in the context of globalisation, liberalisation and other external influences.

At the *intermediate or regional (State) level*, it is a task of Regional Agricultural Land Use Planning, seeking to optimize uses, spelling out the right allocation of land, the right management of land and a fair distribution of its products.

At the micro level of districts, watersheds, village clusters and farms, a highly participatory approach will be called for.

I have already referred to some changes called for in the context of land use planning at the national level. We may now extend our discussion to the regional and local levels.

13. Regional Land use planning

At the regional (State) level, land use planning will have to be in the nature of "*Economic-cum-Environmental (EcE) planning*", interweaving economic, natural resources, environmental and Human Resource Development Planning. For this, the State must be sub-divided into appropriate regions on Agro-climatic-ecological basis. For each sub-region, the overall development strategies should be formulated within an agreed set of guiding principles and an "*Economic-cum-Environmental Action Plan*" should be drawn up. A rigorous Eco-management action plan would involve assessing the maximum utility value of sub-regional land resources by valuation models involving multi-objective linear programming, multi-criteria analysis and trade-off analysis. For accomplishing this, we need professionals with multi-disciplinary training. It should use Geographical Information systems approach based on satellite derived data. The Bhoovigyan Vikas Foundation has prepared the training modules for this purpose. It can share this with the Land Use Planning Boards for jointly holding training programmes.

14. Land Use Planning at Micro Level

Now let me touch on land use planning at *Micro level,* to which I attach great importance. At the micro level, land use planning will be a community-based and farm-based approach. Prof. Swaminathan, who innovated the "*Green Revolution*", has advocated the '*Bio-village model*' *of rural development*, with its thrust on "pro-poor, pro-job and pro-women approach' He calls it the "Evergreen Revolution", which will bring about radical transformation in the countryside. The Bhoovigyan Vikas Foundation has further stretched this model to incorporate an *auto-kinetic development process*, with its hierarchic principle of '*subsidiarity*' and the establishment of '*integrated economic circuits*' involving circular flows, chain effects and recycling ratios.

It is a holistic village cluster approach, incorporating the principles of the PURA concept. It can be operationalised through a massive Land Care movement for bringing about '*Rural Renaissance*'. In order to move towards such Rural Renaissance and operationalise participatory planning, the Land Use Boards must network with a number of local NGOs. The Bhoovigyan Vikas Foundation has prepared a project proposal for "*village cluster development planning*", which while retaining the basic principles of eco-development, emphasizes the promotion of increased avenues for rural non-farm employment. This will stem from an 'auto-kinetic model' of development, for better satisfying the basic livelihood and the material needs of the rural population, through appropriate technologies.

The micro level planning, as envisaged here, should emerge from a "*Technocratic-Academic-Democratic Mix (TAD Mix) Approach*", adopted in the model of Kundrakudi development in Tamil Nadu. It will be a partnership approach in research-cum-action mode, involving the technocrats in government, the academic community and professional NGO's working in tandem with local Panchayats and community-based organisations.

15. Towards Convergence and Synergy

It is obvious that given the range of land use policy measures that need to be implemented at the different levels—national, regional and local—and the cooperative effort needed on the part of various agents—namely the government, community based organisations and the many individual decision-takers, constituting the large private sector—only a '*synergetic approach*' can bring about an *Agricultural Land Use renaissance*" which the new millennium calls for. This can be greatly facilitated through a *National Land Use Advisory Service*, operated through State Land Use Boards, which will disseminate agricultural information relating to ecological, meteorological and marketing factors, on a location and season-specific basis. This should be linked to State and Block Level Land Use Advisory Services, which will greatly assist farmers in pro-actively organising their activities for precision farming. In this way, the Land Use Boards can serve as "*Inspirational Guideposts*" to farmers in the country.

The task of evolving an appropriate and meaningful land use planning system in the country is challenging, but certainly not beyond the collective wisdom of our people and the scientists. Where there is a will, there is a way.

I may also remind you of another saying: "We must not merely talk; we must also walk."

8

National Land Use Policies and Strategies: The Challenges before the Current Millennium*

In the vision of development projected in '*The UN Millennium Development Goals*' (MDGs), land use does not figure explicitly as a goal. But it is implied in the two related MDG's viz. *Goal 1:* Eradication of extreme poverty and hunger and *Goal 7:* Ensuring environmental sustainability. Land use is also an important instrumentality in the realization of what we call "*Inclusive development*", whose base or bottom line is defined by economics, ecology and equity. Heavy population pressure in the developing countries and the related increased competition from different types of land use have emphasized the need for more effective land use planning and management. Thus, rational and sustainable land use is an issue of great concern to our country today, as we seek to achieve the Millennium Development goals as well as preserve our precious land resources for the benefit of present and future generations.

Now let me briefly outline the Challenges and Tasks in Land Use Planning: It is the maladjustment between human society and its environments, which is the greatest scourge, that we will be facing in the new millennium. According to a Buddhist Philosopher Daisaku Ikeda: "Maladjustment, caused by both human and natural

---

* Lecture delivered in the National Conference on "Space Science and Technology for Geographical Research and Applications" September 16-18, 2005, organised by the Centre for Land Use Management at Hyderabad.

factors, such as land degradation, droughts or famines and their whole nexus of related problems, are bound to shake the foundations of both local and international stability and order. Preventing this disaster and restoring eroded and damaged lands through appropriate land use policies and strategies is a scientific and technical challenge of the first order".

To be tackled at the same time to enable transition to an *ecologically adapted land*, it presupposes the optimization of the following tasks:

(1) A massive increase in agricultural production, both in the medium and long-term, to safeguard a sufficient supply of food for the growing population that we will have at the end of this millennium and the repairing of ecological damage to *use*,

(2) The need for environmentally acceptable ways of thinking, acting and addressing the issues in agricultural development, not merely from a national and regional perspective, but also from an *intensely local perspective,* taking note of Global imperatives, and

(3) Blending the best of modern science with traditional wisdom and the ecological prudence of local societies.

The implementation of the above tasks requires not merely the application of a great deal of science and technology, but also a very high measure of moral/humanitarian solidarity and participatory effort among the rural folk, who are the real stakeholders. All these tasks call for an effort to meet the challenges of a shift to the paradigm of sustainable development.

What does this paradigm shift mean? It means essentially a shift to ecologically-oriented ways of thinking and patterns of action. Such action should proceed not merely from a local or regional perspective, but also from a Global perspective, since the 'Global Village' envisioned by Alvin Tofler in his book on '*The Third Wave*' is now a reality. It means a progressive condensation, as well as integration of time and space and man's tightening bondage to the environment by operationalising a plan for "working with Nature". Such development transition would call for new and future-oriented concepts in precision farming for enhanced productivity and land use change for diversification of livelihood opportunities.

This conceptual shift from recuperative or restoration oriented strategies to sustainable development also draws our attention to the traditional systems of land use and the need for a deepened analysis of indigenous, and ecologically well-adapted farming methods prevalent in our rural societies, particularly in agriculture and animal husbandry. Incidentally, this kind of reorientation is, of late, reflected in developed western societies also, by a movement to "*Return to Nature*" and to the traditional forms of land use and soil management. In the above contexts, the next decade must be recognized as the decade for "*Agricultural Land Use Renaissance*", coinciding with the commitment to the UN Millennium Development Goals. A new awareness and a new consciousness must grow during this period. Spatially-oriented disciplines like Geography and Agricultural Sciences are the main stakeholders, who can bring about this desired transformation and change.

In his book on "*The Pedagogy of the Oppressed*", Freire writes that both "*clinging to the 'local', while losing sight of the 'overall view' and taking note of only a 'bird's eye view', while ignoring one's 'footing or local base' are serious mistakes.*" He insists on the importance of a *balanced view*. In the new millennium, our policies and strategies must constantly move from the local to the global and back, to meet the concrete targets set by our international commitments, particularly our commitment to Goal 8, which is to "*develop a global partnership for development*".

Now let me come to the concept of Relational or contextual Space

Land use refers to the manner of optimally utilizing '*geographic space*' for sustainable development. The term '*geographic space*' refers not only to the visible earth's surface, with its various physical features, land forms and natural resource endowments, but also the relatively non-visible '*human values*' including social relations, culture, hopes, and aspirations of the local community. This is known as "*relational space*" (i.e. the natural environment and its relationship with Man, marked by anthropogenic influences). This concept of Relational or contextual space is well known to geographers and space scientists. It is space where Earth and Man interact, to create a new landscape. Let me remind you of a famous quotation from Vidal de la Blache "*A country or Region is like a medal struck in the likeness of a people*". This is a view of space, which serves as the field for human action with their differential values. It provides a framework for physico-socio-economic planning. Thus land use policies must be seen in the wider context of the interface of '*Earth and Man*'. This *relational context* makes a lot of difference in our perceptions and the developmental thinking process. In the works on land use planning done by many agricultural scientists, and soil scientists, I find that the land use prescriptions are mainly determined by the physical attributes, especially climate, topography and soils, as the term '*land capability*' used in this context very clearly indicates. Studies conducted by social scientists in different parts of the world have, however, tended to discredit this approach as 'oversimplisitic' and observed that environmentally similar areas have been developed in quite dissimilar ways by their inhabitants. This has given rise to the concept of "*human ecosystems*", which has underlined the idea that the human attributes of an area, which include social structures, cropping patterns, ways of life and even the culture and temperament of the inhabitants, play a crucial role in the determination of land use. A concept of "human ecosystems" thus implies the notion that individuals and groups relate to their environments, through their perception or cognition of them. This underlines the importance of inscribing human values into our '*Land use analysis*'. The concept of 'human ecosystems approach', expressed here can be injected into the land use planning concept, only through '*micro level studies*', based on participatory rural appraisal methods.

Integration of Contextualities and Capabilities

The above-mentioned propulsive role of relational space for planning, poses not so much a philosophical problem as a methodological problem in integration. This means that when undertaking planning, we must 'integrate' the *contextualities of space* and the *capabilities of the humans*. This should result from two processes involving different methodologies: (1) The first approach is what may be called *Planning for "Natural Resource Management through Land capability analysis"*. This is achieved through the use of scientific analysis, involving the application of modern technologies like

Remote Sensing, GIS and Mapping to understand the type and quality of the land or 'Contextual Space' for different agricultural and other uses. (2) The second approach is a process of *induction*, trying to distil or extract the essence and common denominators in the past activities of societies, their culture and indigenous technologies, or capabilities which have helped in conserving land. This leads to '*People-centred development*', which means adopting a '*human ecosystems approach*' to land use.

The imperatives and tasks in this *congruent approach* are:

(1) Meeting the challenging needs of today and of tomorrow through Green Revolution and Evergreen Revolution.
(2) Economic viability and enhanced productivity through scientific and appropriate land use policies.
(3) Enhancement and maintenance of the quality of environment.
(4) Conservation of natural resources, particularly soil and water, which form the base of agriculture.
(5) Efficient management of natural resources-Land, Water, Energy, Forests and Biological resources.

Before coming to the vital issues of a national land use policy, one must logically present our Agricultural Development Scenario: in terms of Population, Land, Forest Cover and Employment: But I skip this portion, as I am talking to an audience who are familiar with the existing situation.

Land use policy formulation — is a highly balancing act: the land use debate today is being conducted amidst different theoretical currents, with their different perspectives and aims. The Soil and Space scientists, for instance, look at it as a '*prescriptive problem*'. Technologists, on the other hand, look at it as a '*problem of recreating nature through biotechnology and genetic engineering.* Ecological scientists are concerned about *reducing damage* to our ecosystems. Resource management specialists are concerned with '*conservation problems*' and the allocation of the real costs of resource exploitation. Spatial analysts are concerned about achieving *more rational patterns of economic activities*. Behavioural scientists seek *to reduce the unnecessary constraints on people* and to improve their ability to make effective decisions. Economists would like the problem to be considered *within the global economic systems* and tend to view it in a historical process linked to economic and political structures.

The point is that not only do the aims and methods of explanation differ between the different perspectives, but also in the goals for change stipulated and the means advocated to promote the desired change. This makes the formulation of land use policies for this millennium, a highly balancing act.

Now I come to a critique on the National Land Use Policy outline:

In 1988, the Ministry of Agriculture, Government of India came out with a Natural Land Use Policy Outline and Action Points. Now though dated, the 19 Action Points set out in this document are still valid. It only needs some additions and re-orientations in the context of the staggering and sweeping changes that have come about in the national and international realms. The document confines itself mainly to actions at the national level and does not stretch its arms to the regional and local levels, where land use meets its 'client'—the farmer—and the challenges of implementation. The multi-level planning framework and perspective is lacking. Further, in the context of the winds of change, blowing in the form of globalisation, liberalisation, and privatisation, and influencing our developments in a big manner, it needs additional supporting policies to satisfy the requirements of our society, within its core values and socio-economic requirements. In this sense, the NLPO is a somewhat piecemeal formulation. More than the piecemeal nature of its formulation, it is its policy ineffectiveness that is worrying. One of its recommendations about constituting Land Use Boards at the State level suffers from inherent inadequacies. They are mostly functioning in many States without adequate legislative and technical support, and as we say "*stuck in an insufficient mould*". In the post-modernistic era, the Land Use Boards should emerge as effective "inspirational guide-posts", performing with admirable efficiency and giving a lead to managerial action at regional and local levels.

Land Use Policy at the National Level

Land Use Policy at the National level should effectively respond to the global imperatives of sustainable development within the free market paradigm. It should address itself to six axioms:

(i) Reviving a reasonably sustainable growth;
(ii) Changing the quality of growth;
(iii) Meeting the essential needs for jobs, energy, water and sanitation;
(iv) Conserving and enhancing the resource base;
(v) Reorienting technology and managing risk; and
(vi) Blending environmental ethics and economics in decision making.

The above ingredients of sustainable development are expected to ensure that global environmental protection and national economic growth would proceed hand in hand and without any major conflicts.

Cadastral Scale Mapping for Microlevel Land Use Planning: The Need for a Participatory Approach

Let me now touch on the mapping problem. Large scale maps are useful only for macro planning purposes. On the other hand, agronomists and farmers are looking for micro-variations at the field level. The environmentalists desire such data at the watershed level. The economists prefer the data at regional level for their studies. The works that have emerged so far from soil scientists have use only at the regional or country level. The maps to benefit the farmer at cadastral scale are yet to be generated. Even when higher resolution cadastral scale maps become available, we cannot dispense with interaction with the local farmers in a participatory mode. The Bhoovigyan Vikas Foundation is using the methodology of space-related Cadastral Mapping using PRA methods, advocated by Gordon Conway, George Axinn and Nancy Axinn in the projects that it has taken up. These maps will supplement the maps using remote sensing techniques and assist greatly in micro-level planning.

Towards Convergence and Synergy

"By Agriculture, he meant *proper Agricultural Land Use.*"

It is obvious that given the range of land use policy measures that need to be implemented at the different levels—national, regional and local—and the cooperative effort needed on the part of various agents—namely the government, community based organisations and the many individual decision-takers, constituting the large private sector—only a 'synergetic approach' can bring about the optimal use of agricultural landscapes. The task of evolving an appropriate and meaningful land use planning system in the country is challenging, but certainly not beyond the collective wisdom of our people and the scientists. I end up with a quotation. Jawaharlal Nehru observed in 1948:

"Everything else can wait, but not Agriculture."

9

Sustainable Land Resource Management and Land Use Policy

I feel greatly privileged to be invited as a Resource Person in this National Seminar and look forward to a useful exchange of thoughts on land policy and land use planning.

Friends, we are meeting at a time when our Earth, the one and only living planet in our Solar System is in a great crisis. The latest report on the Inter-governmental Panel on Climate Change (IPCC) is really shocking. Some of the devastating consequences detailed in this Report are:

(i) Sea levels will rise by at least 40 cm by 2100.
(ii) Inundation of lands and homes.
(iii) Loss of up to 88 per cent of Asia's coral reefs, as a result of warming ocean temperatures.
(iv) The Ganga, Brahmaputra and Indus will become seasonal rivers and dry between monsoon rains.
(v) Continuous retreat of Himalayan Glaciers, ultimately vanishing entirely by 2035, if not sooner.
(vi) Continuous fall of water tables—decline by over one-third of the gross per capita of water availability in India by 2050. Rise in water-borne diseases, affecting the health of vast populations.
(vii) Fall in crop productivity, especially in non-irrigated land, as temperatures rise for all South Asia by as much as 1.2 degree centigrade on average by 2040 and even greater crop loss of

over 25 per cent, as temperatures rise up to 5.4 degree centigrade at the end of the century.

Thus a grim future awaits India in the coming century. As against, this we have to weigh our experiences on the planning front, over fifty years of our development struggle. Our planners sought GROWTH as the ultimate goal, Plan after Plan. Growth was the mania and as a result, different forms of growth with fragmented programmes have appeared on the scene. I can count at least eight of them.

They are as follows:

(i) Jobless growth i.e. Growth without employment opportunities.
(ii) Ruthless growth i.e. Growth that has aggravated the inequalities.
(iii) Futureless growth i.e. Growth that has inhibited the development of future generations.
(iv) Voiceless growth i.e. Non-Participatory growth or growth that has deprived the participation of by-passed groups in society.
(v) Rootless growth i.e. Growth that has destroyed the cultural roots of our society.
(vi) Inequitable growth i.e. Growth without redistribution.
(vii) Unsustainable growth i.e. Growth which has been environmentally destructive.
(viii) Dependant growth i.e. Growth without self-reliance.

As we are facing all the dilemmas of this ugly growth, planners have now come with a wider concept of "inclusive growth" i.e. an economic, social and environmental package, which will cure our present maladies. We are at present in a world, fast moving towards globalisation, deregulation and privatization, with the winds of change blowing from inside and outside. Local development efforts are rapidly making headway. We are being pushed forward through scientific and technological developments.

What are the prospects before us? Alvin Tofler in his book on "The Third Wave" had envisioned a 'Global Village', which has now become a reality. Now geographical boundaries have little meaning and we have an "international trade regime", organized by the World Trade Organization—with free trade and investment as its principal tenets—that is dictating our path to development. But it is being sought to be so framed as to favour the developed countries, threatening the socio-cultural fabrics of our traditional agriculture, leaving nearly half of the population of the developing world, who are small farmers, on the verge of being marginalized. Thus with many people rendered 'living on the edge' of a futureless precipice, we are now on the throes of re-defining our policies for the sustainable management of our land resources.

Contextuality and Capability

With these preliminary observations, I now come to the mainstream of our discussion on "'*Sustainable Development and Management of our Land Resources*". To begin with, I would like to clear some conceptual cobwebs.

The term 'Land Use' is not to be understood, merely in the sense of an allocation process—i.e. allocation of land for different uses—but must be seen in a wider context of "*Inclusive Development*", whose bottom-line is defined by economics, ecology and equity. Since it is Man, who is putting the land and its biotic resources to their different 'uses', it has to be seen in the context of the interface of "*Earth and Man*".

Amartya Sen has convincingly argued that the goal of development is to expand people's 'capability' to do things, that they have a reason to cherish and value. His 'Capability Approach' enunciates a theory of 'Value' and 'ethic' for assessing possibility and achievability. His ideas related to 'Capability' has been widely applied in planning in different contexts. I have sought to apply it to Land Use Planning.

Any assessment of Land and its different uses for various purposes must recognize the constraints and opportunities for development. Land use, as determined by scientists, is usually based on a rigorous assessment and mapping of physical (Geomorphological, Soil and Ecological) attributes, using satellite imagery and ground truthing methods. It does not take note of the constraints which are individual or "*farmer-based preferences*", such as culture, traditional knowledge systems, community values and social dynamics. Thus one is a scientific decision-making level and the other is at the 'People's level'.

In the way that land use planning is practiced by scientists, there is a relative neglect of the people-level processes in decision-making. In other words, for establishing a conceptual framework for assessing the determinants of Land Use Policies, a conscious blend of the core ideas related to '*Capability at people level*' with an understanding of the potentials and constraints, emerging from a scientific analysis of Geographic or Space perspective is not taking place. This blend i.e. '*Earth-Man-Space nexus*' is the concept of '*socio-spatial milieu*' i.e. space fashioned by human action. It is *Relational or Contextual Space*, in which people have developed their unique institutional formations relating to social, cultural, economic and political arrangements.

It refers not only to the visible elements of Geographic space i.e. physical features, landforms and natural resource elements, but also to the relatively non-visible human values i.e. social relations, culture, hopes and aspirations of the local community. It is space fashioned by human action. According to a French philosopher, Vidal de la Blache, this space is like "*a medal struck in the likeness of the people*", referring to the anthropogenic influences on the lithosphere. This concept of Relational or Contextual Space makes a lot of difference in our developmental thinking process. In the works on land use planning done by many agricultural scientists, and soil scientists, I find that the land use prescriptions are mainly determined by the physical attributes, especially climate, topography and soils, as the term 'land capability' used in this context very clearly indicates. Studies conducted by social scientists in different parts of the world have, however, tended to discredit this approach as '*oversimplistic*' and observed that environmentally similar areas have been developed in quite dissimilar ways by their inhabitants. This means that the human attributes of an area, which include social structures, cropping patterns, ways of life and even the traditions, culture, habits and temperament of the inhabitants, play a crucial role in the determination of land use. These attributes constitute, what I would call the "*Human ecosystems*", approach—a concept which implies the notion that individuals and groups relate to their environments through their perception or cognition of them. Among the drivers of Land Use/ Land Cover change, the most important are the human beings and this underlines the importance of inscribing human values into our Land Use analysis.

Bridging Determinism and Possibilism: Towards an Adaptive Approach

If we accept this concept of "*human ecosystems approach*", then land use must be seen in the context of "*improving our rural livelihoods*", in accordance with human capabilities, traditional knowledge and cultural traits. That would make all the difference in our methodology of land use planning. It would mean bringing in the concept of an "*Adaptive Approach*", which is quite different from the "*deterministic land capability approach*" of physical scientists. The term Land capability as defined by physical scientists, implies "*optimality*" with reference to physical attributes only. It is a tight-jacketed '*Territorial Control*' of land use. On the other hand, the adaptive approach implies a flexible, workable and balanced approach, weighing various human capabilities and possibilities. It underlines the concept of "*possibilism*". This difference between "*determinism*" and "*possibilism*" must be carefully understood. Let me quote again the famous French philosopher Vidal de la Blache, who said "*There are no necessities, but everywhere, possibilities, and Man as the master of these possibilities is the best judge of their use*". In my view, the '*Adaptive Approach*', which I am advocating, will bridge the deterministic and possibilistic schools of thought and would be quite relevant to our times.

The '*Adaptive approach*' also implies the integration of the good features in our traditional land use methods with the modern scientific methods.

Land Use Planning: Challenges and Tasks

Now let me briefly outline the Challenges and Tasks in Land Use Planning. It is the maladjustment between human society and its environments, which is the greatest problem that we will be facing in the new millennium. This "*Maladjustment*", is caused by both human and natural factors, such as land degradation, droughts or famines and their whole nexus of related problems. Preventing this disaster and restoring eroded and damaged lands through appropriate land use policies and strategies is a scientific and technical challenge of the first order".

It presupposes the optimization of the following tasks:

(i) A massive increase in agricultural production both in the medium and long term to safeguard a sufficient supply of food for the growing population, that we will have at the end of this millennium.
(ii) The repairing of ecological damage to be tackled at the same time to enable transition to an *ecologically adapted land use.*
(iii) The need for environmentally acceptable ways of thinking, acting and addressing the issues in agricultural development, not merely from a national and regional perspective, but also from an intensely local perspective, taking note of *Global Imperatives.*
(iv) Blending the best of modern science with traditional wisdom and the ecological prudence of local societies.

The implementation of the above tasks requires not merely the application of a great deal of science and technology, but also a very high measure of moral/humanitarian solidarity and participatory effort among the rural folk, who are the real stakeholders. All these tasks call for an effort to meet the challenges of a shift to the paradigm of sustainable development, with a "*human face*".

What does this Paradigm Shift mean?

It means essentially, a shift to ecologically-oriented ways of thinking and patterns of action. Such action should proceed not merely from a local or regional perspective but also from a global perspective. It means a progressive condensation, as well as integration of time and space and increasing man's tightening bondage to the environment, by operationalising a plan for "*working with Nature*". Such development transition would call for new and future-oriented concepts firstly in *precision farming* for enhanced productivity and secondly in *land use change* for diversification of livelihood opportunities.

The New Imperatives

Let us now take stock of our new imperatives in agricultural land use planning. The Green Revolution (GR) during 1970's and 1980's, led to the achievement of near self-sufficiency in food production. This was no doubt a distinct gain. Now the Green Revolution is facing a new set of challenges posed by the excessive use of chemical fertilizers and pesticides. It has to be rendered evergreen as emphasised by Dr. Swaminathan.

We are also faced with an imperative to relate our developments to the external factors of globalization, liberalization and privatisation of the production and trade regime. Our priorities today are the need to bring about necessary changes in our policies to negotiate these problems, to enhance production and productivity, and to increase the opportunities for off-farm employment and value addition through agro-processing and other Small and Medium Enterprises.(SME's). The major challenge before us is: how to maintain and enhance the integrity of the natural resource base, while at the same time increasing productivity and value addition.

Bertrand Russel once said. "*One must look into hell before one has any right to speak of heaven*".

When applied in the context of achieving *Sustainable Development*, this means that we must first examine and correct the '*ecological footprints*' left by Man, before building up any model of Sustainable development. If that is so, our topmost priority is to take the corrective steps for checking land degradation and accelerating efforts towards ecological restoration.

Spreading a Land Care Movement

This would call for spreading a Land Care Movement, inscribing some elements of "*Returning to Nature*" and adopting some good features inherent in our traditional forms of land use and soil management. The next decade is a decade for "*Agricultural Land Use Renaissance*". Our national land use and land management policies should address these issues. If the Land Care Movement is to be effectively organised in a vast country like ours, we need to build up an effective "*Land Army*" in each village, by organising local youth as social activists. I also recall that the same idea was articulated by Dr. Akhtar Hameed Khan, a distinguished Administrator turned Social scientist in the 1950's , who advocated the "*Comilla Approach to Rural Development*" in Bangladesh.

Multi-level Land Use Policies

Land Use Policy at the National level should effectively respond to the global imperatives of sustainable development, within the free market paradigm.

It should address itself to Six axioms:

(i) Reviving a reasonably sustainable growth;
(ii) Changing the quality of growth;
(iii) Meeting essential need for jobs, energy, water and sanitation;
(iv) Conserving and enhancing the resource base;
(v) Reorienting technology and managing risk; and
(vi) Integrating environment and economics in decision making.

Our Land Use Policy at the National level should also seek to address—issues such as the role of Biotechnology, Agricultural Technologies in different Eco-systems, Bio-diversity and Institutional Reforms. It should also draw up a broad policy framework in the context of globalisation, liberalisation and other external influences.

At the intermediate or regional (State) level, it is a task of Regional Agricultural Land Use Planning, seeking to optimize uses, spelling out the right allocation of land, the right management of land and a fair distribution of its products.

Regional Land Use Planning

At the regional (State) level, Land use planning will have to be in the nature of "*Economic-cum-Environmental (EcE) planning*", interweaving economic, natural resources, environmental and human resource development planning. For this, the State must be sub-divided into relatively homogenous regions on agro-climatic-ecological basis. For each sub-region, the overall development strategies should be formulated within an agreed set of guiding principles and an "*Economic-cum-Environmental Action Plan*" should be drawn up. A rigorous Eco-management action plan would involve assessing the maximum utility value of sub-regional land resources by valuation models involving multi-objective linear programming, multi-criteria analysis and trade-off analysis. For accomplishing this, the Land Use Boards must be equipped with professionals with multi-disciplinary training. They should use Geographical Information systems approach based on satellite derived data coupled with ground truth verification. The Bhoovigyan Vikas Foundation has prepared the training modules for this purpose. It can share this with the Land Use Planning Boards for jointly holding training programmes. We have already held such a training programme for senior officials in Tamil Nadu in collaboration with M.S. Swaminathan Research Foundation and the Tamil Nadu Agricultural University.

Building an Eco-Economy from the Grassroots

The problems posed by population and environment can be solved according to many experts by creating an environmentally sustainable economy from the grassroots. About this, till now, we had only an abstract notion of what it would look like. But some success stories in local level development have taught us some lessons.

To bring this about, we need to *empower the rural poor*, who have little or no skills. In this context, it is necessary to be guided by the *Precept: "To a hungry Poor Man, give a fishing rod, rather than a fish"*. For development activities sponsored by Government, this precept is quite pertinent. When you provide a fish to the poor, they of course, eat it with relish, and then revert back to their original state i.e. poverty. *So EMPOWERMENT of the poor is the key to their development.*

Empowerment implies that we have to bring into action, a band of dedicated youth, to take the role of social animators and catalysts, to promote rural renaissance. This prospect of bringing our youth as a new factor in our development fabric, is to be seen as a fundamental challenge and change in development planning. The task here is not merely to make the community knowledgeable about the threat to our environment, but to make them really Act. Only action with determination will create change. To bring this about, we need to establish a multi-tiered system, to train youth, impart necessary skills to them and to build suitable *Community Based Organisations (CBO's)*, to secure effective citizen participation.

The first layer of this paradigm will consist of the educated youth consisting of *Scientists, Engineers, Researchers and Vikasis in Society* known by its acronym *SERVIS*. They will act as *coalition builders*, between the members of the Gram Sabha and the Government at the district and block levels.

They, in turn, will be trained by extension agencies and agricultural research institutes at the State level, and will function as the voluntary technical advisors for the grassroots level community. In this context, I may bring to your attention that a dedicated retired Professor (scientist) in Canada Dr. Amarnath Kshatriya has devised a methodology for bringing about such a coalition for rural development. He has already demonstrated this in Canada. He is prepared to work with any group in India . He is a Fellow member with the Bhoovigyan Vikas Foundation and is collaborating with us. Institutions like IIM may take note of this unique opportunity to collaborate with him.

The second level will consist of *unemployed village youth* with some school education, (including school drop-outs), who will be trained in some skills by polytechnics located in every block, to work as social animators in Community Action Planning.

The Third requisite in this paradigm are *supporting structures*, including the Panchayati Raj Institutions and various poly-centric village institutions, as well as knowledge centres like "*Information Technology (IT) Centres*", located in rural libraries/schools for diffusion of knowledge. The entire team with its supporting structures, as envisioned here, will prepare a *comprehensive model of village planning*, incorporating the aspirations and efforts of the local community, so that the plan might be grounded concretely in their own future.

Apprehensions may be raised as to how this can be made to happen. In my view, this is quite possible, if the student power in the universities is fully harnessed, with their teachers also providing the necessary input and guidance.

To enable this, it should be made mandatory for graduate students in every discipline—Physical Sciences, Social Sciences, Engineering, Technology and Management—to spend the final Semester or six months of their education in rural service, studying the potentials and needs of a selected village cluster of about 20 villages, at the end of which they will prepare a report laying out an "*Operating Vision*" for Microlevel development.

Road Map for the Future

Road map for the future must have its own *Earthcare Policy Institute* to decide its policies to halt the pillage economy. I shall now indicate what some scientists have opined to restructure the global economy and to make it compatible with the Earth's eco-systems, so that a sustainable economy can evolve and save our earth from impending disaster. Lester Brown, President of Earth Policy Institute advocates a paradigm shift toward an *Eco-economy*. In the new economy, wind farms will replace coal mines, hydrogen-powered fuel cells will replace internal combustion engines and cities will be designed for people, not for cars. Another scientist Jeffrey Sachs, Director of Earth Policy Institute at New York, has opined that by achieving the *Millennium Development Goals*, it would be possible not only to reduce poverty and inequality, but also lessen environmental problems, such as air pollution and deforestation. It is for the developed and developing nations to choose the right path in their different developmental contexts. The right kind of policies have to be hammered out for each country which would offer, not only a vision of an *eco-economy* but also frequent assessment of progress in realizing that vision. This means each nation.

During the last six years since the Bhoovigyan Vikas Foundation was founded, we have been vigorously advocating for the setting up of an Earthcare Policy Institute in our country, which would take a holistic and integrated view on the conservation and strengthening of Earth's vitality.

This institute has been envisaged to function as a high-performing knowledge institution, *establishing in due course, linkages with surrounding countries and emerging as the* "Regional Centre for South-South Cooperation" *and engaging in* "Ecological Diplomacy" *to save our plundered planet*. We hope we will succeed in our effort. If this Trans-Disciplinary institution is established it will help to evolve sound Earthcare policies cutting across the Lithosphere, Hydrosphere,

Biosphere and the Atmosphere of our planet. This will help evolving policies to tackle environmental degradation related to industrial pollution and the long-*term climate change associated with massive use of fossil fuels and the global sustainability of the world's ecology in* unison to achieve this goal and let me hope that our dream will materialise.

I end my speech with two quotations One from T.R. Lawrence:

> "All men dream; but not equally
> Those who dream by night
> In dusty recesses of their minds
> Wake in the day to find that
> it was vanity;
> But dreamers of the day are dangerous men
> For they act their dream with open eyes
> To make it possible"

The second quotation is from Dr. Jeffrey Sachs, Director of Earth Policy Institute in Columbia University , New York:

> "Let the future say of our generation that we sent
> Mighty currents of hope, and that we worked together
> to heal the Earth".

IV
Information Technology

10

The Fourth Era of Information Technology Development and its implications for Geography

In this technical presentation, I propose to reflect on the Fourth Era of Information Technology Developments and its implications for our discipline. It is in the nature of a futuristic vision, and seeks to set out a hope, a wish to quote 'John Keats', a hope "beyond the shadow of a dream". I start with some recollections.

In our student days, we followed the conventional geographical research techniques and went through a grueling experience to obtain our Ph.D. degree. It involved labourious data collection, equally labourious cartographic exercises, overlaying the maps drawn on tracing paper to identify spatial correlations, and delineating distinctive 'areal units' for choosing our sample villages for the study. This first stage of the exercise was a labourious and crude method. Even the data collection was a frustrating experience. Even today, when I think of my experience as a research student in the University of Madras, I tremble and shiver and recall with surprise how I waded through all those hurdles.

---

* Keynote address Delivered in the Deptt. of Geography, Delhi School of Economics on 21-02-03.

But today, thanks to the efforts of the National Informatics Centre, the National Sample Survey organization, the State Bureaus of Statistics and Economics etc, the building up of the database has been rendered much simpler. Developments in Information Technology has been an evolution, with clearly distinguishable stages. In the 60's, the Quantitative Revolution came in Geography, with the Principal Components Analysis, Factor Analysis and other statistical techniques, emerging. It was a big change, which was a highly labour-saving device in combining numerous variables into a single index.

Then came the Main frame Computer Revolution in the middle of the 60's, which underwent many improvements in technology. In 1986, I was invited to an Expert Group meeting on 'Information Systems for Local and Regional Planning in Developing Countries' at Kawasaki in Japan. In this meeting, we took stock of the evolution of information technology and identified three stages of computer revolution.

The first was the "transaction processing era", in which large payrolls accounting, inventory and order processing systems were rendered simpler.

The second era was the development of "Management Information Systems", with its emphasis on developing data base, useful for managers for organising operating data as well as transaction data, and for developing a variety of reports for use by managers at various levels.

The third era of computer revolution emerged, with its emphasis on the concept of "Decision-Supporting Systems or what is also called, End User Computing (EUC)" using micro-computers, which has now become in common usage.

We are now in the Fourth stage of development, which is described as the "Fusion of Technologies Era" by Dr. Moni and other scientists. This has emerged through the new technology of Geomatics, which is the science and technology of gathering, analyzing, mapping, interpreting, distributing and using geographical information for various applied aspects of planning and development.

The term 'fusion of technologies' is a beautiful expression and most appropriate to describe our current exercises in research, because Geomatics encompasses a broad range of technologies, that can be brought together on a common spatial reference system, to create a detailed and understandable "spatially juxtaposed picture" of the physical world and our place in it. These technologies include:

(i) The G.I.S.
(ii) Global positioning
(iii) Remote sensing
(iv) Digital mapping; and
(v) Cadastral surveying

These technologies could now be used to help resolve, both area (i.e. land with its biodiversity coverage) and human development problems and to seize opportunities or entry points for planning and decision making in numerous areas. They include:

(i) Producing all the basic maps to create the picture of an area's geography, environment and socio-economic characteristics.
(ii) Identifying soil and land degradation and other problem areas
(iii) Land care and environmental management
(iv) Land cover information and planning of forest regeneration and conservation
(v) Determining the extent of loss of our bio-diversity and planning appropriate conservation strategies
(vi) Planning utility infrastructures and their management
(vii) Natural resource exploration, development, monitoring and management
(viii) Development planning—rural and urban land use
(ix) Coastal zone management and mapping
(x) Land Information System (LIS) through the combination of digital images and cadastral boundary data; and
(xi) Planning and administration of transportation and telecommunication systems, and perhaps many more.

Thus, Geoinformatics has become the ultimate data integrator, an ideal tool with which we may integrate and analyse spatial information. The science of Geoinformatics, thus provides a single window to the wealth of Earth Science Knowledge. The internet provides the delivery of that knowledge in a client-focused and consistent manner. It also provides multi-disciplinary integrated solutions to problems related to the natural as well as the developed environment. It provides not only professional skills, but also stimulates lateral thinking and creativity. While the G.I.S. and Remote Sensing, no doubt have become a great boon to researchers, I must also caution some pitfalls, especially on the user front. For instance, most of our scientific organisations, using the GIS and remote sensing dynamics, like the National Remote Sensing Agency, the National Bureau of Soil Survey and Land Use Planning etc. are preparing a number of District Atlases for the diagnosis of problems to aid Development planning. But these maps are done at 1:50,000 scale. These are now mostly in the nature of academic exercises only barring perhaps those exercises commissioned by implementing agencies. Land use planning and development rigorously using these valuable techniques, and legally enforced has not yet started in a serious sense in the country. It can happen only when these exercises percolate down to the grass roots level, and the Scientists work in partnership with farmers, user groups and community-based organisations in a participatory endeavour. This means that we need to work with maps at the cadastral scale (1:5000), by combining . and integrating these technologies with relevant ground surveys and socio-economic surveys. In other words, G.I.S. and other techniques should no more be restricted to confine their analysis and research within the confined space of their laboratories and indulge only in macro-analysis, but should fan out and spread their wings, as a '*Lab-to-Land*' and a '*Macro-to-localism*' movement and get integrated with rural problems at the grass root levels.

I must also sound another word of caution and that is, that these techniques should no longer remain "investigator-centric". There is a tendency among academics to keep techniques and knowledge to themselves ' 'as secret', in an effort to heighten their own image as "well known Specialists", and remain in that status as long as possible. This tendency, in my opinion should be condemned. The need of the hour is to disseminate every piece of acquired knowledge to the benefit of others and enlarge our research in application areas, by which the bridge between data and decisions could be built up. In this context, I would strongly advocate that every Geography Department should adopt a 'cluster of villages' in the vicinity of their campus, as their laboratory area, and through intensive applications and studies in that area, play a crucial role in stimulating rural regeneration and renaissance. Even a few exercises of this kind will have their enormous 'demonstration effect', as one candle will light the other. Let us remind ourselves about the 'Tachai Experience' of China, where Mao's clarion call, "Go to Tachai and Learn", had a massive spread effect.

Already a number of new projects and methods in Geoinformatics applications are appearing in technical journals. Recently, Dr. Jack Massey, a geographer in Adelaide University (Australia), has advocated a method of identifying "spatial cognition surfaces", as a new approach to interpret spatial distribution of various phenomena. All these studies are worth studying to evolve new methodologies.

I would end my presentation by saying that there is a very long way to go for geographers in this Century, to realize the vast potentials of Geoinformatics as a research tool. I am sure that they will constructively avail off this win-win situation to their best advantage.

11

Leveraging ICT and Digital Geography for Building Sustainable Societies in Rural Space

Our present century is characterized by three major innovations in the area of Technology and Planning. These are:

(i) Developments in ICT, which have made communication and dissemination of information rapid and revolutionary;
(ii) Digital Geography, which has rendered possible, a '*basket of Technology applications*' in a swift and speedy manner for planning and developmental tasks.
(iii) Social survey techniques, with their participatory appraisal methods, which have brought interactive and user interface solutions possible.

What is still missing is a *synergy* of these applications, which can be replicated across the country in a right '*mix*'. I shall come to this mix at a later stage of my presentation. The theme of my presentation is how to bring about this synergy into the '*Planning for sustainable societies in viable rural space*'.

I understand that a few years ago, the Government of India issued instructions to invest 3 per cent of their budget for building ICT capacities. It means an investment of several thousand crores of rupees. Had this amount been used with a coordinated vision and strategy, followed by action through a roadmap, by this time, we could have created a magnificent ICT infrastructure and its related developments in our rural areas.

This is not to belittle the numerous experimentations, pilot projects and demonstrations, which were there during this period. However, they were all sporadic and uncoordinated experiments. I must, however, mention a few recent initiatives *viz.*, the initiative of NIC towards data applications for development through its DISNIC programme; the initiative of NRDMS of Department of Science and Technology through neighbourhood mapping, by training school students and that of M.S. Swaminathan Research foundation through establishing '*Knowledge Information centres in Rural Areas*'. All these experiments must be seen as noteworthy innovations to bring together a '*Technocratic, Academic and Democratic Mix*', a phrase which I coined in the 1970s in the context of the successful rural experiments in *Kundrakudi* and *Sukhomajri.*

Mr. Sameer Kochhar has done a *Yeoman* service by bringing us all together for a peer-to-peer interaction in this two-day meet and to showcase a rich content of successful experiments from different states. While these experiments must go on at the individual and pilot levels, to ensure their sustainability and replicability, some kind of institutional mechanism should be devised to consolidate the gains of these initiatives and to develop a '*National Strategy for E-governance*', followed by a Road-map to reach the goals within an acceptable timeframe.

With Mr. Kochhar's initiative and drive, I am confident that we can build up a "*Think-tank*" i.e. an *E-powered National Centre for Inclusive Development,* as a planning and coordinating body, outside the Government structure, that can undertake independent studies on its own, as well as evaluate and monitor the initiatives, measure the benefits thereof and take the country fast-forward towards a '*Knowledge Society*'. The present time seems propitious for transforming rural India through micro-level planning. This is what I will be emphasizing in this presentation.

At home, a new government has taken over and some fresh thinking is brewing. Our Prime Minister is calling for a new deal for *Rural India*. Our President is emphasizing on the *Provision of Urban Amenities in Rural Areas (PURA)*. The Tenth Plan strategy is emphasizing the generation of rural employment. *But how are we to achieve all that?*

Transforming Rural India is a challenging task. In our current thinking, it has to be along a '*triple bottom line*' i.e. along economic, ecological and social fronts. To achieve such an inclusive development, we need the support of a '*Fusion or convergence of Technologies*', besides poly-centric institutional structures with different foci of interest that can take our villages along the development path, *fast forward in time*.

There needs to be a total '*inversion*' of the planning process, in which our villages, grouped into economically viable village clusters, can transform themselves into '*growth engines*' and harness the latent power and resources of the village community. This will be possible through an *Auto-kinetic Model of Development planning* engineered through participatory approaches as well as through the application of sophisticated technologies like ICT, Remote Sensing, GIS, GPS, Biotechnology, Green Technologies etc.

During the last more than half a century of our 'Learning Curve', we tried to bring about rural development through a large number of loose and fragmented central and centrally sponsored schemes handed down from above. But the very large number of such schemes and the "organizational pluralism", which they entailed, encouraged corruption and spelt their total failure. The new approach to micro-level sub-national planning must address itself to five critical challenges, which are:

(a) poverty reduction;
(b) employment and value added income generation at household, village, block and regional levels;
(c) widely shared growth;
(d) sustainable natural resource management through integrated water resource management and farmer-relevant land use planning strategy; and
(e) strategic investments in people through education, health, connectivities and water supply and sanitation.

Since the 70's, the concept of rural development has undergone many changes. It is now "Inclusive Socio-economic Development", which inheres in it, the tasks of 'poverty reduction', 'employment generation', 'empowerment', 'equity', 'sustainable development of the natural resources', besides the provision of basic minimum services. It has to be generated from "within", by unleashing the "Capillary Mechanisms" in the village situation, with people deciding their course of development and government supporting it. In this conception, the core tasks of rural development will include the fuller use of land and water resources without destruction, modernization of farming by extending processing and marketing activities, building non-farm and allied agricultural activities, setting up institutions like cooperatives and other forms of social capital, empowering panchayats and women and improving health and education services. We therefore argue, that in order to bring about 'Inclusive Rural Development, with people's participation nexus, the growth impulses need to be structured and built up at the level of "clusters of villages", in a highly integrated and effective manner. This line of reasoning implies a new perspective and a much deeper '*economic and social content*', of development addressed to both public delivery and receiving sides. It is much more than ensuring merely a viable size of settlement for supporting a particular amenity or service. In this conception, the effectiveness of a 'cluster' at grass root level depends not so much on the size alone of the population brought together, but on the degree of cohesiveness and integration among the constituent villages and social groups, quality of local leadership and capacity of rural institutions to bring the rural weak and poor within their fold. It is here that understanding the village as a part of rural neighbourhood assumes importance in planning for development. This new concept of rural development can be translated into action only through 'social animators' (committed NGO's) and 'change agents' (researchers) joining hands with local bureaucracy/technocracy and local people and their institutions. It has to be seen as a joint endeavour of various "Partners in Progress", with clear goals (Fig. 11.1). Very aptly, Dr. M.S. Swaminathan, renowned agricultural scientist has called for the declaration of the year 2006-07, as the year of agricultural renewal and adopting a holistic approach to Evergreen Revolution i.e.: advancing crop productivity in perpetuity, without any ecological and social harm. He has also proposed a concept of watershed centred developmental initiatives in rural areas naming it

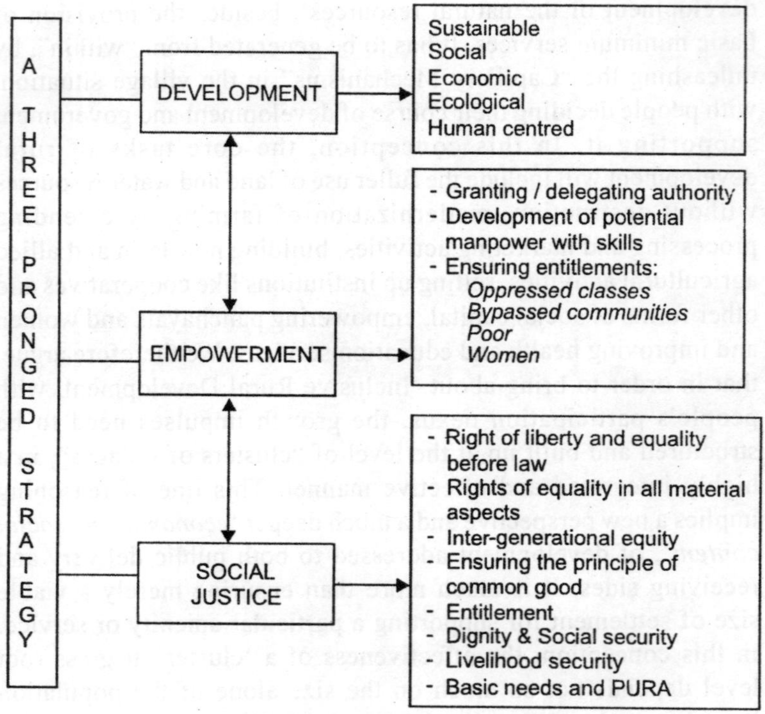

Fig. 11.1: Partners in Progress

"Rainbow Revolution" for generating synergy among various activities.

The Delineation of Village Clusters (VCs)

The first initiating step for creating "*Inclusive Socio-economic Development in the Rural Areas*" would be the delineation of 'Village Clusters (VCs)' as the grass root level units for rural planning and development. The ideal rural planning units would be the "*Cohesive Rural Community*", which can be delineated by taking into account the social, economic and spatial inter-relationships, as well as the power structure of the community. The Village Clustres (VCs) are thus envisaged as 'Community of Interest Areas (CIAs)', in which people's association and social contacts will be of a voluntary nature, with people being drawn together by common interests in economic affairs, trade, social interests for recreation or religion etc. The focal point for each 'Community of Interest Area (CIAs)' will be a 'central place' (focal village) of viable population size, already performing some area-wide functions such as school services, medical services, retail services, social and recreational services, business services and transport services.

A viable *Village Cluster* would be the lowest area level unit for planning and development, covering 5 to 6 contiguous villages, having a distance span of 4 to 6 kilometres and with a total population of about 8,000 to 10,000. The *Village Cluster* is only a structural component of rural development. In order to make it a really "*functional unit*", dynamism has to be infused in its central place and the constituent villages through various forms of '*Connectivities*', '*flows*' and '*iterative interactions*'.

The central places will be the '*nodal/focal*' points, which are endowed with a certain minimum threshold of population, endowed with necessary infrastructure and services and having the potential to propel activities relevant to development and radiate development impulses to surrounding villages.

The four critical 'connectivities' to induce development are: (i) *Physical Connectivity* or road and transport and power connectivity to bridge distances; (ii) *Electronic Connectivity* to increase communication through media and digital opportunities; (iii) *Knowledge Connectivity* through education and imparting of skills and extension services to provide information, technology, and increased understanding; and (iv) *Market Connectivity* to link rural products to markets. The inadequate presence of these connectivities have been seen as the "major irritants", or obstacles to development in our rural areas and their removal is considered vital for rural transformation.

Simply providing connectivities will not do. They should be rendered *dynamic* through 'flows', which have to be consciously induced in four directions viz. vertical, downward, horizontal, and circular. The 'Vertical Flows' will provide bottom-up connectivity to higher order centres of activity for processing of commodities produced in primary villages and information on local needs and preferences, area priorities, targets, local problems and constraints. The 'Downward or Top-down Flows' will provide macro-micro linkages and information flows relating to policies, priorities, targets, guidelines, budgetary and technical support. 'Horizontal Flows' will establish inter and intra community information flows and interactions. 'Circular Flows' will enhance the recycling-ratio within the villages, adding income to the village and bringing about a circular movement of commodities from the primary villages to their processing centres and the return movement of finished products to consumer centres.

'Interactions' constitute the vital component of this dynamic system and is closely related to both electronic connectivity and knowledge connectivity. It involves (a) the interaction of the *people's institutions with government's institutions*; (b) the interaction of people, as individuals, with their own institutions, like the Village Panchayat and Community-Based Organizations (CBO's); and (c) people to people informal interactions through their social organizations. Thus, the planning intervention envisaged as "Cluster Development" and sought to be operationalized here through the nodes, connectivities, flows, and interactions, in space will ensure participatory development and enable bridging the rural-urban gap, providing urban amenities in rural areas (PURA) and enhancing the quality of life and livelihood opportunities for the rural people.

The Operating Vision, Tactics and Planning

"Where there is no vision, the people perish" is a well-known planning axiom. It is only with a clear operating vision of objectives, thrusts, tactics, and programmatic interventions that any village cluster (VC) can hope to meet its '*tryst with destiny*'. Initially such a vision will never be totally explicit. It is latent, as a community's attitude towards itself and its aspirations are not easily visible. With iterative interactions with different sections of the community, however, this can be discovered with some clarity. With the modern tools of analyses, the vision that is latent could be objectified in Table 11.1

Creating an economically viable agricultural and industrial base for the village on the lines of an Auto-Kinetic Model of Development is seen above (Fig. 11.3). By auto-kinetic development, we mean a process by which the auto-centric and auto-dynamic forces of development can be unleashed, which will release the inner urges,

Table 11.1: Holistic Planning for a Village Cluster Concepts and Key Dimensions

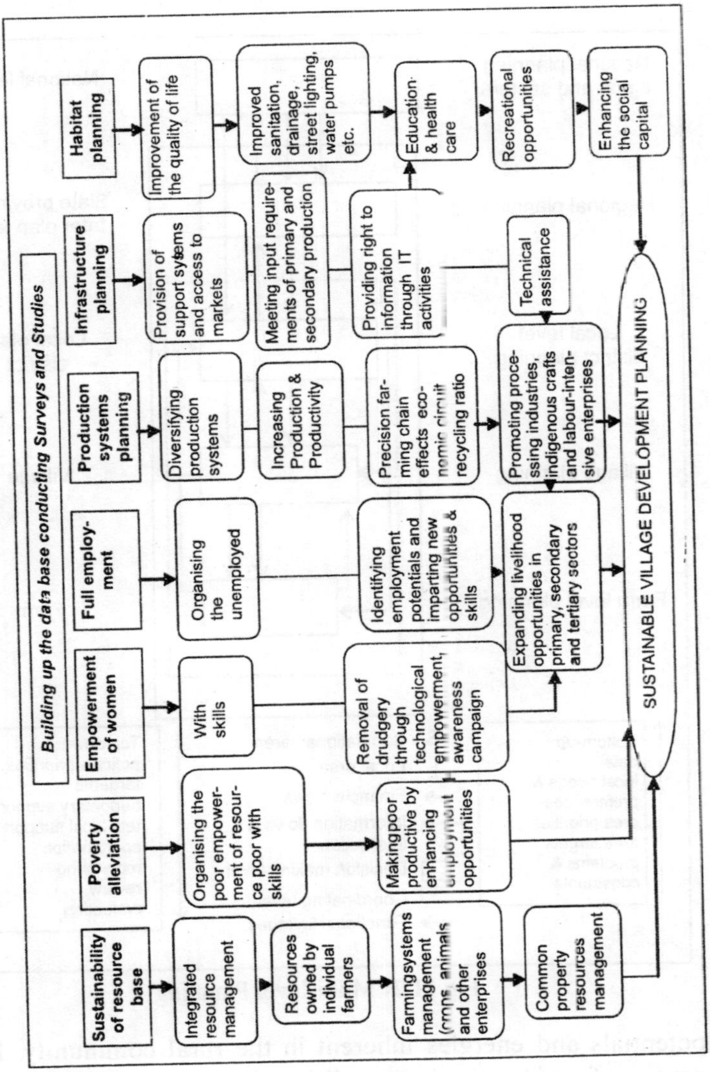

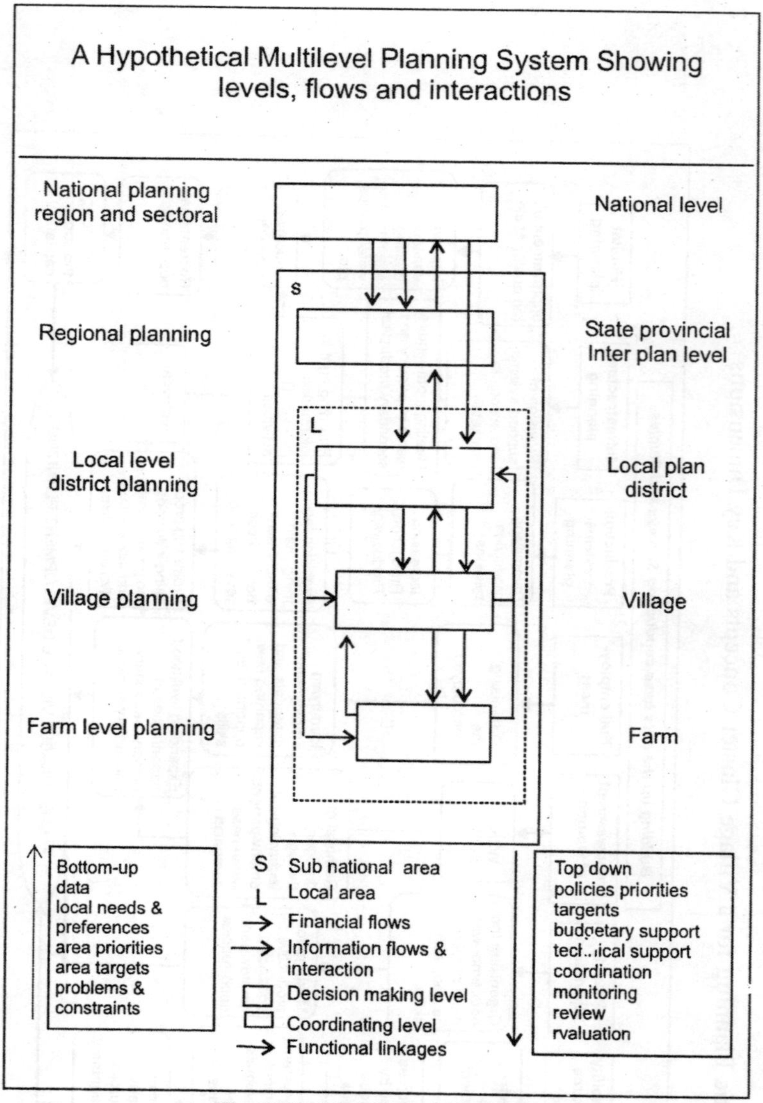

Fig 11.2: Multi-level Planning

potentials and energies inherent in the rural community. It is a process of engineering the overall development of productive forces, with the objective of better satisfying the basic livelihood and the material needs of the rural population, based as far as possible on a

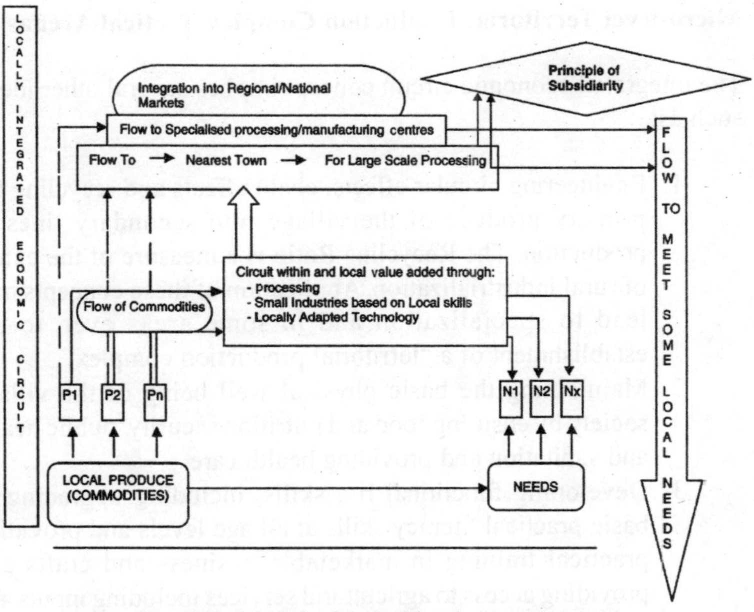

Fig 11.3: Model of Auto-kinetic Development

more intensive utilization of local resources, by means of locally adapted and locally controllable, labour-intensive and small-scale technologies. It is the same as the Gandhian concept of Village Swaraj with the capillary mechanisms in place, for initiating "development from within". It points to a definite method for augmenting rural incomes.

The auto-kinetic development process rests on the hierarchic principle of subsidiarity, which implies what can be done at a particular spatial level must be done at that level only. Thus we should seek to establish processing/manufacturing units at higher level, only when the existing technologies and skills do not allow these to be performed in a satisfactory fashion and at a justifiable cost in the lower spatial level. In the auto-kinetic development approach, the basic objective of achieving the full development of the natural resources and human skills available in the villages can be secured only by establishing "locally integrated economic circuits".

Micro-level Territorial Production Complex-Tactical Arenas

The integrated economic circuit concept implies several other ideas, such as:

1. Engineering circular effects, chain effects and recycling the primary produce of the village into secondary lines of production. The Recycling Ratio is a measure of the extent of rural industrialization. Application of these concepts may lead to specialization and in some areas even to the establishment of a "territorial production complex".
2. Maintaining the basic physical well being of the village society by ensuring food and nutrition security, public health and sanitation and providing health care.
3. Developing functional life skills, including upgrading of basic practical literacy skills at all age levels and providing practical training in marketable business and crafts and providing access to agricultural services including inputs and markets.
4. Another tactical arena would be breaking the isolation of the village and establishing external support relations. This could be established through fostering the necessary institutional relations with the public and private sectors and adapting the development programmes initiated by the government, to suit the local specificities and needs, forging extended business contacts, e.g. for securing bank loans to fund local projects and promoting the village public image.
5. Leveraging *ICT Through Bottom up Explosion* is one of the major tactics for transforming the village into a knowledge-based society. This would include setting up of: *Rural Info Centres in Clusters of Villages, i.e.* (Telephone and Fax Services) and—Rural Knowledge Centres *(Computer and Internet Facilities)*

In this manner, agricultural information for precision farming through extension agencies and price signals from neighbouring market centres could be accessed by the rural community. The 'Hub and Spoke Model' for a knowledge communication centre is illustratively indicated in Fig. 11.4.

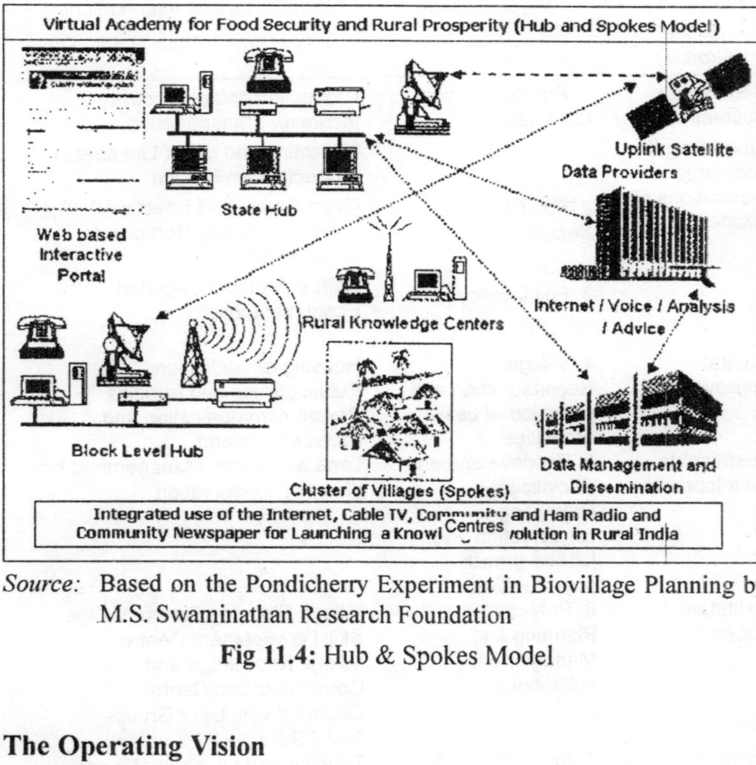

Source: Based on the Pondicherry Experiment in Biovillage Planning by M.S. Swaminathan Research Foundation

Fig 11.4: Hub & Spokes Model

The Operating Vision

The arching dimensions of the operating vision may be visualized in five broad groups viz. community sustenance; habitat improvement; sustainable development; institutional support; and social awakening. Each group has been further elaborated to indicate the major thrusts and further detailed into 'enabling programmatic interventions', for actuating the 'Vision'. These are outlined in Table 11.2, which illustrates in a nutshell, the planning framework for the study.

Programme Content

Successful implementation of the Holistic Village Cluster Development strategy requires complex decentralized matrix

Table.11.2: Holistic Village Cluster Development Project: Operating Vision

Objectives (Broad Groups)	*Major Thrusts*	*Programmatic Interventions*
Community Sustenance (upgrading the economic foundations of village life)	1. Agri-Production Complex	Production and productivity increase, Transportation, Marketing and credit Linkages, product diversification
	2. Food and Nutrition Security	Grain Golas; and Effective PDS; Livestock/Poultry/Horticulture development
	3. Full Employment	SME's through Integrated Economic Circuit
Habitat Improvement	4. Village Reconstruction and provision of basic amenities	Housing rehabilitation, Public utilities and facilities, Power, communication and transport systems
Sustainable Development	5. Ecodevelopment (Biovillage)- Promoting conservation and job-led growth opportunities.	Land and Water Management; bio-diversity conservation
Institutional Support	6. Poly-centric Planning and Management Institutions	Village Planning Forum, Village Skill Development Centre, Village Knowledge and Communication Centre Cooperatives, User Groups, And CBO's.
Social Awakening	7. Social Rebuilding (through social animators)	Training and education for social effectivity, Literacy training, Training for women/youth, Land Army, Barefoot Doctors/Engineers/Technologists etc.

structures, with permanent mechanisms for vertical and lateral integration, a combination of specialist and generalist skills, institutional leadership, social intervention capability and systems management. The methodology and programme content would include the building up of the databases for decision-making through secondary and primary surveys and selected analysis and studies conducted by using PRA methods.

The evolution of Information Technology has already gone through three stages of computer revolution. The first was the "*Transaction Processing Era*". The second was the era of development of "*Management Information System*". The third era was the "*Decision Supporting System or End User Computing*".

We are now in the *fourth era of development,* which is the "*Development Applications Era*" involving the synthesis and fusion of technologies taking development fast forward towards the knowledge century. With appropriate "*Organizational Mechanisms*" in place, to advance our research, development and policy fronts, India can certainly become a leading country in the World of Technologies.

12

Tools and Mechanisms for ICT-led Agriculture Sector Planning and Rural Development

Evolution of Information Technology

Developments in Information Technology have been an *evolution*, with clearly distinguishable stages. In the 60's, the *Quantitative Revolution* came in Geography, with the Principal Components Analysis, Factor Analysis and other statistical techniques, emerging. It was a big change, which was a highly labour-saving device in combining numerous variables into a single index. Then came *the Mainframe Computer Revolution* in the middle of the 60's, which underwent many improvements in technology. One may identify *three stages* of computer revolution in the evolution of Information Technology:

(i) *The first was the "transaction-processing era"*, in which large payrolls accounting, inventory and order processing systems were rendered simpler.
(ii) *The second era* was the development of "*Management Information Systems*", with its emphasis on developing database, useful for managers for organizing operating data as well as transaction data, and for developing a variety of reports for use by managers at various levels.
(iii) *The third era* of computer revolution emerged, with its

emphasis on the concept of "*Decision-Supporting Systems or what is also called, End User Computing (EUC)*" using *micro-computers*, which is now in common usage.

We are now in the *Fourth stage of development,* which is described as the "*Fusion of Technologies Era*". This has emerged through the new technology of Geomatics, which is the science and technology of gathering, analyzing, interpreting, distributing and using geographical information for various applied aspects of planning and development.

The term '*fusion of technologies*' is a beautiful expression and most appropriate to describe our current exercises in research, because Geomatics encompasses a broad range of technologies, that can be brought together on a common spatial reference system, to create a detailed and understandable "*spatially juxtaposed picture*" of the physical world and our place in it. These technologies include:

(i) The G.I.S.
(ii) Global positioning
(iii) Remote sensing
(iv) Digital mapping; and
(v) Cadastral surveying

These technologies could now be used to help resolve, both area (i.e. land with its bio-diversity coverage) and human development problems and to seize opportunities or entry points for planning and decision making in numerous areas. They include:

(i) Producing all the basic maps to create a picture of an area's geography, environment and socio-economic characteristics.
(ii) Identifying soil and land degradation and other problem areas.
(iii) Land care and environmental management.
(iv) Land cover information and planning of forest regeneration and conservation.
(v) Determining the extent of loss of our bio-diversity and planning appropriate conservation strategies.
(vi) Planning utility infrastructures and their management.
(vii) Natural resource exploration, development, monitoring and management.

(viii) Development planning—rural and urban land use.
(ix) Coastal zone management and mapping.
(x) Land Information System (LIS) through the combination of digital images and cadastral boundary data; and
(xi) Planning and administration of transportation and tele-communication systems, and perhaps many more.

Thus, Geoinformatics has become the ultimate *data integrator*, an ideal tool with which we may integrate and analyse spatial information. The science of Geoinformatics, thus provides a *single window* to the wealth of Earth Science knowledge. The internet provides the delivery of that knowledge *in a client-focused and consistent manner.* It also provides multi-disciplinary integrated solutions to problems related to the natural as well as the developed environment. It provides not only professional skills, but also stimulates lateral thinking and creativity. While the G.I.S. and Remote Sensing, no doubt, have become a great boon to researchers, I must also caution some pitfalls, especially on the user front. For instance, most of our scientific organisations, using the GIS and remote sensing dynamics, like the National Remote Sensing Agency, the National Bureau of Soil Survey and Land Use Planning etc. are preparing a number of District Atlases for the diagnosis of problems *to aid Development planning*. But these maps are done at 1:50,000 scale. These are now mostly in the nature of academic exercises, only barring perhaps, those exercises commissioned by implementing agencies. Land use planning and development (legally enforced), rigorously using these valuable techniques, has not yet started in a serious sense in the country. It can happen only when these exercises percolate down to the grass roots level, and the scientists work in partnership with farmers, user groups and community-based organisations in a participatory endeavour. Our Hon'ble Prime Minister has recently called for a movement towards rural regeneration and renaissance. This means that we need to work with maps at the cadastral scale (1:5,000), by combining and integrating these technologies, with relevant ground surveys and socio-economic surveys. In other words, G.I.S. and other techniques should *no more* be restricted to confine their analysis and research within the confined space of their laboratories and indulge only in macro-analysis, but should fan out and spread their wings, as a 'Lab-to-Land' and a 'Macro-to-localism' movement and get integrated with rural problems at the grass root levels.

Application to Agriculture Sector and rural development: I may now illustrate how to bring in *unified effort* to stimulate the delivery and receipt of information and other services in the agriculture sector at the grass roots level. Besides ICT and Geomatics as tools, for development in any sector to take place, we need also mechanisms for knowledge sharing and effective flow of information. For achieving *Inclusive and Integrated Rural Development* (comprising *Economic, Ecological and Social Aspects*), they constitute a major challenge.

Mechanisms in the agriculture sector are, really speaking, the *agri-support activities* and refer to those infrastructure and institutions that facilitate or are in some sense, basic to the carrying on of a wide variety of economic activities. The *progressive agriculture. **The latter will*** **include the provision of inputs for *precision farming, processing and marketing* activities.** For deriving the maximum advantage from these various *mechanisms* or *agri-support activities*, each one of them must be effectively coordinated with all the others of different types within each locality, in order that the complementarities among them may be fully exploited.

Different Kinds of Mechanisms

What are these mechanisms that we are talking about? In *Agricultural Economics*, we distinguish between two categories of *Infrastructure Mechanisms* viz. *Capital Intensive* and *Capital Extensive*. *Capital Intensive Mechanisms* include:

- (i) Irrigation and Drainage Systems;
- (ii) Transport Facilities;
- (iii) Storage Facilities;
- (iv) Processing Facilities;
- (v) Utilities : Electricity and Power, Drinking Water System, Gas etc.

Capital Extensive Infrastructure include

- (i) The specialized research and education services i.e. new knowledge that is developed and transmitted for improving agricultural productivity through extension mechanisms. These constitute Technical Information;

(ii) Some social services delivered such as Plant and Animal Protection and Soil Conservation Techniques;
(iii) Credit and Financial Institutions, which provide the essential funding for modern agriculture; and
(iv) Health and Education for Human Resource Development.

In the developing world, most of these activities are carried out by the public sector, and the allocation of funds to them calls for criteria to determine the levels of operation, best calculated to promote agricultural growth.

There is also a '*third category of mechanisms*' which include: the formal and informal institutions of a legal, political and socio-cultural nature, that affect agricultural economic activity including such items as general law and order, property and land rights and personal safety. By and large, Governments in Developing Countries have been concentrating on the problems of land tenure and agrarian-reforms. The choice of institutions for the operation of these mechanisms, formal or informal, in most developing countries will be based on the socio-cultural values of the societies.

Central Mechanism-Extension

The *Central Mechanism* in the agricultural development process is "*Extension*", *both in terms of technology transfer and human capital development*. The earlier view about '*extension*', related to technology transfer for increasing agricultural productivity. This viewpoint ignored its role in human resource development, particularly the needs of many low-resource farmers operating on marginal land and the needs of small farmers, women farmers and land less families. Since the number of extension agents to farmer's ratio is much lower in the developing countries, *extension mechanisms* in these countries are quite inadequate and inappropriate for the problems to be solved. Now, we are at a crucial juncture in human history, when the benefits of revolutionary new technologies are within the grasp of rural communities. The needs and aspirations of the neediest and marginalized communities could be accommodated by leveraging the full benefits of ICT's through "*Rural Knowledge Centres*".

Local Level Mechanisms

At the local level, what matters is how the *Delivery and Receiving Mechanisms* are organized. Here, decentralization and the roles of *local bodies (Panchayati Raj Institutions), Community-based organizations, Volunteers or Self-help Groups and Cooperatives* are the driving forces. They are the essential mechanisms, which are involved in the action process of planning and implementation. These mechanisms are also meant to induce some important *values*, such as self-help, diligence, cooperation and participation; to foster village leadership and participatory organizations and to improve the physical and social environment of villages. They are the *Action Agents*, which play the role of *Change Agents*. They are "*Partners in Progress*" in advocating and bringing modern science and information and communication technologies, which have tremendous potential for accelerating development. With their support, the ICT-led development will become a powerful mechanism for reducing knowledge-gaps and increasing knowledge-sharing among farmers. They are the front-line agencies for increasing productivity and boosting growth in rural areas. They promote what is called "*Development from Within*".

In this context, it is important that for effective transfer of technologies, we must associate the academics, particularly in the disciplines of agriculture, economics and a spatially-oriented subject like Geography. Here I must mention that in the 1930's, Prof. Dudley Stamp in England motivated students and teachers and prepared land use maps for the entire country of Great Britain. For a vast country like India with more than 6,00,000 villages, if we can motivate and harness the teacher and student power for various types of activities like Biodiversity Mapping, Land Use Mapping, Neighbourhood Mapping, Natural Resource Mapping, using IC technologies including RS, GIS and GPS, we can lead the country to *Rural Renaissance*. This will be a great venture to initiate a low cost solution to Rural Development Planning. Here, the cooperation of the Citizens, Change Agents and the Government Support are the crucial variables.

The new ICT will only bring *Knowledge Connectivity*, but such knowledge should be absorbed by the Rural Community and rendered dynamic through '*Flows*' of different orders—*Vertical Flows* providing *bottom-up connectivity*; *Top-Down Flows* providing *macro-micro linkages* and *Horizontal Flows* establishing *inter and intra community information flows*.

'*Interactions*' constitute the lifeblood of this dynamic system, encouraging poly-centric institutional interactions with a large number of "*Partners in Progress*", which is the *hallmark of integrated rural development*. The *Bhoovigyan Vikas Foundation* has proposed a '*Village Cluster Mechanism*' to bring about an "*Auto-kinetic Model of Development*", *which will induce flows and interactions* through '*Circular Effects*', '*Chain Effects*' and '*Recycling*' *as well as linking production, processing and marketing activities in the agriculture sector* (Fig. 12.1). This model, would bring together the *Community of Geographers and Earth Scientists* in an attempt at *Holistic Village Cluster Development* (Fig. 12.2).

It is time that the full potential of the ICT's is harnessed to serve the specific needs of poor farming communities. New Information and Communication Technologies along with Geoinformatics can accelerate broad-based rural growth, and by increasing awareness, help make it a central pillar of overall development strategy. Only then will we be able to achieve *Sustainable Development* in the truest sense of the term, and possibly a *Sustainable Future* for all.

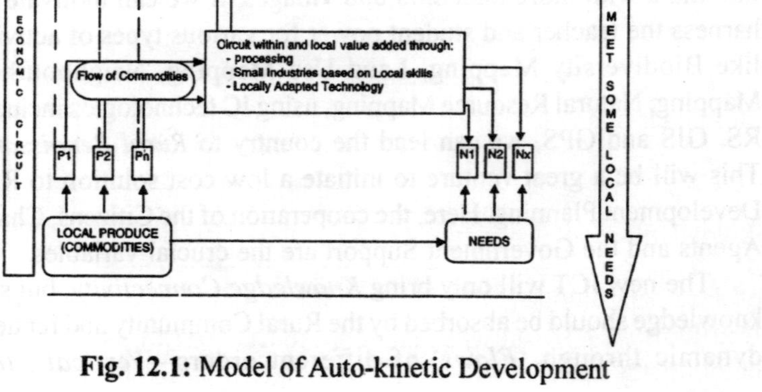

Fig. 12.1: Model of Auto-kinetic Development

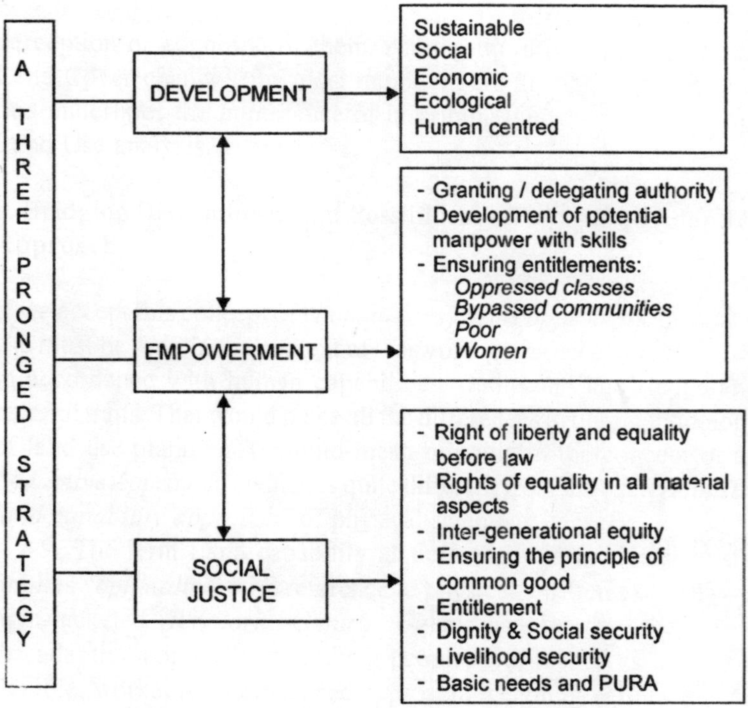

Fig 12.2: Holistic Village Cluster Development

V
Sustainable Development

V

Sustainable Development

13

Earth Crisis and Women's Role in Sustainable Development: A Social Scientist's Perspective

"Sustainable development is the buzzword of this New Century. It falls between several disciplinary tools. Besides its technology dimensions, we have to view the subject in wider human terms, both male and female.

The Approach

Currently, our intellectual processes for change are somewhat confused. On the one hand, there is the conservative outlook, which sees all past development policies and strategies in a negative way and advocates an effort to turn the clock back, or simply to continue in the same direction, as things are going today, with "growth" as the major thrust. On the other hand, there is the debate between thinkers of varying shades, who have some understanding of what has gone wrong, but are unable to agree on what can put things right. It is against this background of dilemma that we have to sharpen our debate on sustainable development, natural resources management and the role of women in remedying the problems. Our objective is to achieve an ecologically sustainable economy, i.e. "eco-economy". Based on

---

* Key Note Address prepared for delivering in the Holy Cross Women's College, Thiruchirapalli, Tamil Nadu 15-17-March, 2003 International Conference on "*Sustainable Development and Management of Resource*".

a balancing act of economic, social and environmental planning and management, which ensures minimum damage to ecological processes.

Such an approach would lead us to think strictly about scientific natural resources management, which while preserving the traditionally gained knowledge, skills and culture of local and regional communities, will also integrate and benefit society by benign modern technologies. In this context, the term "Ecological Modernization" *has* emerged as a "*New Paradigm of Placing Limits to Growth*". It signifies an approach towards achieving development based on technology, scientific knowledge and increasing productivity, but within the carrying capacity of our supporting eco-systems.

What Has Gone Wrong?

In the first place, let us ask the question: what has gone wrong? To answer this question, we have to examine the present state of our earth in relation to its life-supporting systems of air, water, land, forests, bio-diversity, energy and the man-made interventions in our habitat and the production and processing of our materials economy. The consequences and ravages of human action, if recounted, would constitute a long catalogue of environmental degradation. I have short-listed about 14 consequences of human actions (Appendix1) which have threatened the well-being of the earth in different parts of the world, which have adversely affected our ecosystems in varying degrees and are posing a major threat to life on earth. Scientists are concerned that some trends of this human action will reinforce each other i.e. causing the "synergistic effect", which are often irreversible. Lester R. Brown, Chairman of the Earth Policy Institute in Washington, U.S.A. has recently observed. "Over this last quarter-century or so, many battles have been won, but the gap between what we need to do to arrest the environmental deterioration of the planet and what we are doing continues to widen. Somehow we have to turn the tide".

My contention is that our present crisis has emanated from our lack of harmony with nature and our non-adherence to the laws governing nature. What are these laws governing the natural system and from which we can derive some lessons? I would list a few of them:

(i) Setting limits to human behaviour and action, within a moral and ethical value system, which is a mode of self-control, which thinkers like Mahatma Gandhi advocated. *Ghandhiji called it by the expression "Swayalamban"*;

(ii) Setting limits to growth by curtailing extravagant consumption, which Gandhiji called by the expression, 'Sarvodaya';

(iii) Organising the society in accordance with the principle of 'self-management by objectives', which Gandhiji called by the term "Village Swaraj";

(iv) Minimising entropy, which is a thermodynamic principle for curtailing non-renewable energy use;

(v) The principle of recycling our materials economy, by redesigning and replacing the current linear "flow-through model" with a "circular model", that emulates nature, thus rendering the man-made wastes regenerative;

(vi) Following the principle of symbiosis i.e. co-existence of differing species of organisms and systems to their mutual benefit.

I shall not dwell at great length on these laws. But this brief introduction was necessary to understand what has gone wrong.

Where is the Road to Sustainable Development?

To come to more practical, "down to earth" interpretation of sustainable development, one has to proceed from a negative approach to get a positive answer. For instance, we need to ask and answer with under the present regime? Is the current precision, such questions or "Is crop system sustainable lifestyle of the people sustainable? Is our *current pattern of human settlements* sustainable? Anyhow modern technology is the answer?

If answers are 'No', the question is how the sustainability can be improved? It has to be through cooperation, collaboration, and participation to get things moving in a development process, with 'conservation' as our focus and sustaining the improvements, so as to ensure that the resulting benefits from various developments are effectively maintained and equitably shared. Obviously, this means that local participation and cooperation, coupled with efficient governance at local, regional and national levels have to be secured. If sustainable development has to make any headway in practical and operational terms, it should be from the bottom i.e. from the village, to a cluster of villages and then upwards to towns and citces. It should then converge into the 'top-down approach'.

It involves a tri-fold participation in development by:

(i) The stakeholders (the state, local/The civil society (community based sub-local/regional);
(ii) Organisations, professional organisations, non-governmental organisations, teachers and students; and
(iii) The Market place (i.e. small/medium sized enterprises, multinational corporations and financial institutions)

Participation in development by all these three major entities, in unison can transform and re-organise our present village, which can be made to withstand the onslaughts of globalisation and liberalisation. This would lead to a movement towards *'sustainable development, sustainable lifestyles and sustainable consumption'*, which is the only hope for meeting the challenges of our present Earth Crisis. In this context, I would confine myself only to what teachers and students can accomplish in this vital transformation of the society.

Sustainable Development and Transformational Change Through Education

In the wake of globalisation, liberalisation and privatisation that is transforming the world economy today, a totally *new educational architecture* is warranted. This must be based on four major re-orientations:

(i) The new education system must be marked by vision, values and ethos suited to the new millennium;
(ii) Educational institutions should play a catalytic role to instill human values and to develop students into self-reliant, self-confident and self-generating personalities.
(iii) The educational curriculum must change in character and content. It should not be confined only to classroom teaching;

but the students at the graduate and post-graduate levels must be encouraged to go to our villages, conduct field-studies and understand the realities of rural living and the rural society. They should play a key role to spearhead a movement for bringing about societal change;

(iv) The students must be encouraged to learn from natural systems. Our present ills in environment and society emanate from the non-adherence to the laws of nature, for which I would emphasize a "*systemic approach*". The present system continues in a direction, unmindful of its objectives and values and has the risk of becoming cancerous. Alternative models are available from some success stories and they should be put into action. To cite a few success stories: The VANRAI model of Mohan Dharia, the Ralegaon Sidhi model of Anna Hazare, the Bharatiya Agro Industrial Foundation's model for sustainable livelihood, the M.S. Swaminathan Foundation's model of Biovillages in Pondicherry and the Kundrakudi model of Rural Development in Tamil Nadu which I had christened as Technocratic, Academic and Democratic mix (Tad-Mix). The Bhoovigyan Vikas Foundation's Auto-Kinetic model of Rural Development is a more comprehensive model, which takes into account economic development, population, environmental security and employment opportunities.

This alternative model of development should come about as a '*Rural Renaissance Movement*', through a spatially-oriented strategy of development. This implies a big transformational change in rural India. To move in this direction, every educational institution—college or university—should adopt a cluster of 5 to 6 villages in its neighbourhood as its laboratory area and undertake a "*holistic village cluster planning*". They should study the selected villages through various participatory techniques, including the '*participant observation technique*'. After creating the data base, the planning should be based on the auto-kinetic model of development, with its underlying concepts of enhancing "*re-cycling ratios*" in the village, establishing "*integrated economic circuits*" in village clusters and the promotion of agro-industries in accordance with the Gandhian principle of "*subsidiarity*", and conforming to Christaller's concept of hierarchical planning of economic activities and social services. This model of economic development will be complemented by Eco-development, on the lines of the Biovillage Model of Dr. M.S. Swaminathan Foundation. It is our belief that only such an approach of spatially integrated, hierarchically conceived, participatory and ecologically oriented development would trigger off a process of rural renaissance in the country. This also implies the adoption of precision-farming and integrated land use planning, based on the "*fusion of technologies,*" which is now possible with our scientific advancements in geospatial and ICT tools of development.

For achieving transformational change in rural India and meeting the challenge of increasing growth, a three-fold strategy is suggested, consisting of (a) leveraging information technology for rural transformation, (b) leveraging biotechnology for sustainable growth and (c) linking farmers to remunerative markets for rural partnerships, enhancing competitiveness. The first strategy for instance, will bring about knowledge-based empowerment of the Indian farmer and will also enable creating infrastructure for agri-supply chain management and rural distribution. The second strategy, that of leveraging biotechnology, will support large scale farming and social forestry, together with watershed management, to create additional avenues of income to the rural poor. The third strategy of linking farmers to remunerative markets will provide the fillip to the food processing industry and lead to value addition to the farmers, by opening up remunerative opportunities to them.

To move in the above directions, the corporate sector companies should develop a "*commitment beyond the market*". The Indian Tobacco Company has followed a strategy on these lines, by establishing '*e-choupals*' in a number of villages, which has led to transformational change in rural India. This example is worth emulating.

Women's Role in Sustainable Development

As the major protectors of natural resources and most concerned with their proper utilisation and sustainability for future generations, women rank as the foremost guardians of our environment. 'Eco-feminism', which underlines the distinctive relationship existing between women and environment must now receive greatest importance in Eco-management, as women have extensive knowledge about natural resources. We must remember that when environmental degradation occurs, women will be the greatest victims.

There are four areas, where women's role in sustainable development will be quite significant. These are:

(i) Agriculture management;
(ii) Forest Resource management;
(iii) Water resource management; and
(iv) Energy resource management.

During my UN assignment in Nepal, I noted that female labour contribution was maximum in agricultural management, particularly in the dry and wet-terrace management on mountain slopes and marginal lands in all agriculture-related activities, such as the field preparation and ploughing, including crop-sowing, weeding, harvesting, manure supply and food processing. According to a survey by the International Centre for Integrated Mountain Development (ICIMOD) , women's labour contribution is 8 to 10 fold higher than that of men. In the area of forest resource management, women happen to be the main collectors of fuelwood and fodder for daily consumption in rural areas.

Multiple actions are necessary to ensure the role of women in forest resource management and decision-making. Evaluations made of women's role in Joint Forest Management have brought out their constraints in the decision-making process. These include:

(i) Traditional role;
(ii) Social and cultural barrier;
(iii) Limited experience of women in effectively voicing their interests owing to illiteracy; and
(iv) Logistic constraints like time and double work burden.

It is in this context that the concept of 'eco-feminism' must emerge as an effective movement to create awareness among women about new technical knowledge regarding natural resource management for sustainable development. In this context, it is necessary to educate women about the new approaches for enhancing their role in sustainable development.

Some critical issues in this context are;

(i) Increasing women's access to productive resources;
(ii) Increasing women's participation in decision-making;
(iii) Enhancing capacity-building in women;
(iv) Equal employment opportunities and equitable remuneration for women;
(v) Building gender-sensitive data bases;
(vi) Assessing and combating the impact of environmental degradation, particularly drought and desertification; Integrating the value of women's unpaid work in the resource accounting mechanism; improving women's literacy, education, nutrition and health ; and
(vii) Eliminating persistent negative stereotypical images of women through media, education and socialisation patterns;

There have been success stories by some NGOs, who have been dealing with issues of women and environment. Some of the NGOs like *ADITHI* in Bihar and the Self Employment Women's Association (*SEWA*) have done commendable work, the former focused on the traditional fishing community, and the latter on water campaign. Let us hope that a favourable environment will be soon created, where women will get all the opportunities to prove their mettle in promoting sustainable development, sustainable lifestyles and sustainable consumption and saving the Earth from its impending catastrophe.

It was only when I was posted as an International Civil Servant in Nepal, that I could grasp the full dimensions of the role being played by women in sustainable development. During my visits to the various parts of this mountain country, I could closely observe the huge workload of women in mountain agriculture. I could see that there was a large information gap on gender issues in that country, because there was not much researched literature on the subject, though ICIMOD is now filling up this gap. Since promoting District Development Planning was the major task that had been assigned to me by FAO, I decided to include in the training programmes organised for decentralised planning, a module for training rural women. Bio-diversity conservation and ethnobotany were chosen as important entry points to capture indigenous knowledge. ICIMOD is undertaking Case Studies on Community-Based Conservation Plant Resource Management of medicinal plants, non-timber forest products, agro-forestry, home gardens etc. I do not know if women's colleges in our country have introduced Ethnobotany in their curriculum of studies. If they have not done so, this should be done, so that the indigenous knowledge systems could be studied and biodiversity conservation could be undertaken as an important development activity in the villages chosen for Holistic Planning, a point which I emphasized earlier.

I end this address by quoting the famous English poet John Keats, 'Let this be a hope beyond the shadow of a dream'."

Appendix-1

(i) A third of the World's crop land is losing topsoil, that is undermining its long-term productivity.

(ii) 50 per cent of the World's range land is overgrazed and deteriorating into desert.

(iii) The World's forests have shrunk by about half, since the dawn of agriculture and are still shrinking.

(iv) Two-thirds of oceanic fisheries are now being fished at or beyond their capacity. Overfishing is now the rule, not the exception.

(v) Overpumping of underground water is common in key food-producing regions.

(vi) Over the last 3 decades, global average temperature has risen from 13.99 degrees Celsius in 1969-71 to 14.43 degrees in 1998-2000, a gain of 0.44°C. If CO_2 concentrations in the atmosphere double pre-industrial levels by the end of this century, reaching 560 ppm, the temperature will rise by 1.4-5.8°C. This rise will lead to more extreme climatic events—record heat waves, the melting of ice, rising sea level and more destructive storms.

(vii) In the Arctic Ocean, sea ice is melting. The ice sheet has thinned by 42 per cent and it has shrunk in area by 6 per cent. A recent study by two Norwegian scientists projects that within 50 years, this ocean would be ice-free during the summer. Sea level would rise leading to the oceans expanding at the expense of continents, with consequences such as inundation of coastal areas, salt water intrusion and beach erosion.

(viii) Water scarcity is increasing, as each year some 80 million additional people are staking their claims to the Earth's water resources. One manifestation of emerging water scarcity is dry rivers. Several of the World's major rivers now either run dry part of the year, failing to reach the sea or have little water left, when they get there e.g. Amu Darya in Central Asia, the Yellow River, in China, the Nile in Egypt, the Jordan in Israel, the Ganges in India and the Mekong in Indo-China.

(ix) Falling water tables due to over pumping is another phenomenon being witnessed in many parts of the globe. Northern China is drying out on account of depleting aquifers, leading to the abandonment of wells. In Punjab, the "food basket" of India, the water table is falling by 0.6 metres per year, forcing farmers to drill deeper and deeper. In the Southern Great Plains of U.S.A., practicing irrigated agriculture with water pumped from the Ogallala aquifer with little recharge, the farmers are forced to return to Dryland farming.

(x) With excessive demand on fisheries, the world is witnessing the collapse of fisheries all over—inland, coastal and oceanic fisheries and commercial fishing is under great threat. Damage to coral reefs, a breeding ground for fish in tropical and sub-tropical waters, is also taking a toll.

(xi) The Earth's forested area, estimated at 5 billion hectares at the beginning of the 20th century, has now shrunk to 2.9 billion hectares. This forest loss is concentrated in developing countries. The environmental effects of deforestation are becoming all too visible, with scores of countries suffering from disastrous flooding and alteration in the rainfall cycle, with its effects on the natural vegetation.

(xii) World-wide, almost half of all grasslands are lightly to moderately degraded and 5 per cent are severely degraded. Fodder needs of livestock in nearly all developing countries now exceed the sustainable yield of range lands and other forage resources. In India, for instance, the demand for fodder in 2000 was estimated at 700 million tons, while the sustainable supply totalled just 540 million tons.

(xiii) With an estimated 36 per cent of the world's crop land now losing top soil at a rate that is undermining its productivity, our food security will be at risk, if this trend continues. Some examples of stressed relationship, which has affected the biological base are:

- Top Soil loss, declining yields and the abandonment of crop land experienced in Kazakhstan in Central Asia and in Ethiopia, Kenya and Somalia in Africa.
- Shrinking crop land area in China's coastal provinces, with crop land being lost for the construction of factories, roads and expanding cities.
- Increased frequency of dust storms in China. Yield losses due to soil erosion in African countries, bringing down the grain harvest by 8 million tons or roughly 8 per cent.
- Desertification of crop land in Algeria.

(xiv) Another major threat is the one concerning the disappearance of species. The archeological record shows five great extinctions, since life began on Earth. We are now in the early stage of the sixth great extinction. Unlike the previous ones, which were caused by natural phenomena, this one will be of human origin. The International Union for Conservation of Nature (IUCN) has pointed to the large increase in the "critically endangered species" in all categories—bird species, mammal species, fish species, amphibians etc.

14

Population and Environment: Facing the Challenges

Introduction

I congratulate the Department of Geography of Dayanand Girls College for their initiative in organizing this timely National Seminar on "*Population and Environment-Challenges and Opportunities*". It is timely, in the sense that practically throughout the developing world, population is growing, while per capita arable land and water resources are shrinking.

Friends, inspite of vast developments in *Technology and Development* techniques, the developing countries of the world today are in a deep-seated and multi-faceted development crisis, mainly characterized by three major challenges: i.e. (i) *Population explosion* (ii) *Environmental degradation* and (iii) *Economic stagnation*, which is a consequence of the above two.

This National Seminar has very aptly chosen the issues in population and environment as the central thematic focus for our discussions to the issues of population and environment. Inevitably, the discussion will centre around the factors conditioning Man-

---

* Key Note Address delivered in the Department of Geography, Dayanand Girls College, Kanpur (U.P.) 27.11.2004 National Seminar on "Population and Environment".

Environment interface and how the increasing population numbers, advances in technology, and social organizations have led over time, both to an escalating level of impact on and manipulation of the environment by man.

The Population Explosion

Among the various factors influencing the development process, the potential population explosion is almost a nightmare. It has tremendous repercussions on every nation's physical resources and social services. Even as population continues to grow, the habitable portion of the planet is shrinking, owing to ecological degradation, and the rural population is bound to face greater and greater land scarcity. Whole families will be constrained to subsist on a mere one hectare of land or even less. Poverty will reach unimaginable dimensions. This is the scenario that emerges from a global analysis of the historical trend of population growth in the developing countries, as visualized by many world organizations.

When I was with the United Nations and serving in the various Sub-Saharan African countries in the 1990s, the well-known African Leader, Robert S. McNamara, in an address to the *Africa Leadership Forum*, made a very distressing statement, which I quote: "In these countries, population is growing exponentially, with a sharp decline of the extent of arable land per person to less than 0.3 hectares, with acute food insecurity and hunger, resulting in famine conditions, nutritional deficiency and hunger and leading to migration and even death. A child born today in Sub-Saharan Africa faces a bleak set of statistics. The odds are 1 in 10, that he or she will not live for more than a year and the child's mother will die giving birth. As for life expectancy, the child can expect to live for only 50 years–25 years less than children in the developed countries".

Our situation in India is not so bad; but still we face the problems of food insecurity, nutritional deficiency and hunger, in a context of regional inequalities, sharp social differentiations and problems relating to the degradation of our natural resource base. Almost every year, this vicious cycle of under development spins in different ways and at different speeds, in different regions of our sub-continent. Despite some achievements in population control, the nexus between poverty and environmental degradation poses a critical threat to our development in this 21st century.

The Environment and the Ecological Yardsticks

From population problems, let me come to the environmental issues and challenges facing us in this century. The quality of the environment depends on man's keen perception and careful utilization of natural resources. When technology remained primitive and population was comparatively small in relation to land area, pressures on the environment, in terms of its capacity to meet the competing resource needs were not great. But conditions have changed.

During the latter half of the last century, the World economy expanded seven-fold along with disproportionate consumption of material resources and adoption of lavish lifestyles by the developed countries. International trade also grew rapidly. The economic indicators showed remarkable progress. These developments were, no doubt, different from country to country, and especially between the developed countries and developing countries. But while the economic growth indicators showed progress, the ecological indicators tell a different story, by *every ecological yardstick.* This is reflected in the current state of our eco-systems that supply our food i.e. forests, range lands, fisheries and crop land, as well as the minerals and raw materials that support our industrial economy, marked by mismanagement of natural resources, their reckless exploitation and reduction in our natural resource stocks. Today, at the beginning of this 21st century, we commence our journey on the planet, with a dubious legacy i.e. with a heavily depleted natural capital base and a highly deficit '*ecological balance sheet*'.

The "Tragedy of the Commons" and a belated realization

Let us take stock of what the human beings have done to the Earth. It is a story of "*colossal environmental destruction*", to which we woke up only in the early 1970s. This led to a late realization of the need to work towards the common goal of "*Saving our Planet and Saving our Progeny*". Earlier in 1798, Thomas Malthus had warned that population, when unchecked, will outrace the Earth's ability to provide sufficient food. Although the neo-Malthusians have sought to soften the argument by holding out the possibilities of effective population control and technological innovations, with our natural resource base under constant threat, the case for the revival of our plundered planet, seems weak, at least in the short-run.

The Triple Bottom Line for Sustainable Action

As human numbers and the scale of their activities increased, the pressure on fragile eco-systems also increased. At the global level, several International conferences have been discussing these problems, since the first one at Stockholm in 1972. The real breakthrough, both conceptually and on the policy front, came in 1987 when the World Commission on Environment and Development (The Brundtland Commission), called for a new style of development that meets "the needs of the present generation, without compromising the needs of the future generations". More conferences followed, one in 1992 at Rio de Janeiro, in 2001 at New Delhi (BVF), and another in 2002 at Johannesburg. The greatest contribution of all these multilateral discussions was in highlighting the need to simultaneously address developmental and environmental imperatives and in defining developmental objectives along a 'Triple Bottom Line' i.e. *Economic, Social and Ecological*, which is now referred to by planners as "Inclusive Development". The Triple Bottom line and the objectives implied therein are indicated diagrammatically as follows:

It became clear that without better environment stewardship, development will be undermined, and without accelerated development in poor countries, environmental policies will fail.

The Role of Technology and an Experience in Transition from Sustainability to Unsustainability

At this stage, physical scientists responded by devising new technologies that could ameliorate problems caused by the narrow focus on economic growth and productivity. According to them, technology would solve all these problems. But this was not true. Technology also led to some adverse results, as evidenced by the third

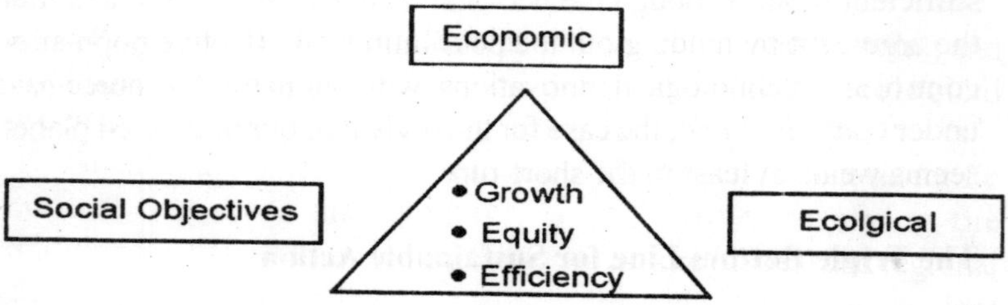

Triple Bottom Line

- Empowerment
- Participation
- Social Mobility
- Social Cohesion
- Cultural Identity
- Institutional Development
- Social Equity
- Poverty Reduction
- Population Control

* Ecosystems integrity
* Carrying capacity
* Natural Resource Management
* Bio-Diversity Conservation
* Global Issues

generation problems caused by the Green Revolution. This is evidenced by:

- Soils and Streams contaminated by fertilizers
- Air (Atmospheric Systems) polluted with wastes
- Crops and forests ravaged by disease etc.

Now the question is what can we do about the problems that result from the intensification of resource management and the expanding scale that often accompanies it? An alternative view in this context suggests that reverting to traditional science and technology i.e. '*Indigenous Knowledge*' or '*Traditional Knowledge and Practices*' will be rewarding. This means that whatever is valuable in this knowledge should be brought into the mainstream concerns and programmes of development, thereby enriching both the modern and the traditional systems.

In this context, I am reminded of an experience in '*transition from sustainability to unsustainability*', which came to my notice, when I was with the FAO of the United Nations and posted in the Sub-Saharan African countries. This incident was narrated to me when I visited the Sahel region of Africa—in what is now Mali and Niger.

The climate of this region is very dry with average rainfall less than 600mm per year, which is a lower limit for most agricultural crops. The local ethnic group living in this region called 'Marka', are experts in the cultivation of certain varieties of native rice. They have been cultivating this crop since pre-historic times. They have learnt this art to perfection. They know when to plant and what varieties to plant, taking note of climatic fluctuations. Their decisions are influenced by environmental clues and the performance of different varieties of rice, which have different vegetative periods, different adaptations to various flood depths, flood timing, pH tolerance and fish predation. But this knowledge is kept as '*secret*' and known only to the select Marka group. This group has not only maintained a specific ethnic identity, but also developed a special '*Social Relations system*' with other groups and devised some "*buffering mechanisms*" to tide over the potential bad times. Into these regions, through international aid, a Regional Development Project was introduced, which brought about a change of cultivation from indigenous rice varieties to the Asian variety *ORYZA SATIVA,* which is more marketable and has a higher yield, but requires considerable amounts of water. This proved to be a disaster. As a result of this experimentation, the traditional system got eliminated and along with it, the "*Secret environmental and social knowledge of the community*". A large portion of the native groups had to abandon the cultivation system and became poorer.

I am narrating this story not to say that we should abandon all modern technology and revert to rice cultivation, along the lines of the traditional 'Marka' in Africa. It is only to indicate that technology itself has to adapt to traditional knowledge, where such knowledge has its own intrinsic merits, which can be tapped, protected and improved with innovations and practices.

Implementation Aspects

(a) The 'adds-on' versus 'integrated' approach

This discussion has made it abundantly clear that a '*holistic, cooperative, multilateral and partnership approach*', needs to be taken to halt the looming ecological and other catastrophies, with due deference to ethics, values and the promotion of justice and equity in consumption and lifestyles. Persistent poverty, environmental degradation, deforestation and desertification can no longer be ignored. The challenges and trends in this direction can only be reversed by *concerted action.* They call for appropriate planning interventions at the local, regional, national and international levels. Here I would stress that a *unified approach to planning and decision-making* is called for by the nations of the world. This implies a vital change or departures from the current operating procedures and programme planning. Many countries have sought to address environmental concerns as "*adds-on*" to development policy-making. This means a *casual approach to meet 'environmental concerns'*, after the core of decision-making has been made. The difference between adds-on and integrated approach is that in the former, 1 + 1 is equal to 2, but in the latter, it is 11.

(b) Restructure the planning mode at different spatial levels

The adoption of the '*Integrated Approach*' will also correct a fundamental error in our planning methodology, in which the costs of environmental and social damage are not embedded in the decision-making process from the beginning. This correction in methodology implies that we have to prepare '*systematic area plans*' at the regional and local levels, besides the macro planning at the national level. The two kinds of planning at the sub-national levels that the Bhoovigyan Vikas Foundation (BVF) has been advocating in this context are:

(i) Holistic Village Cluster Planning at the local level, with participatory approach as the basis; and
(ii) Regional Economic-cum-Environmental Planning at the regional level, with ecosystems approach as the basis.

For both, the BVF has methodologies, which will help in setting appropriate regional and local priorities, promoting positive synergies to promote adverse environmental impacts and mainstreaming the environmental issues in national policy planning. To achieve this, strong political will and determined action are needed, as these are radical departures in planning. Academic and professional organizations have a great role in devising area-specific methodologies and operationalizing them. They should relentlessly advocate for these drastic changes and reforms in development planning.

We need to deal not only with domestic or national issues, but also with international concerns, like climate change, rising sea level, dying coral reefs and disappearing species. In this respect, humanity, now more than ever, truly stands at a defining moment in history. The tide in the affairs of '*Earth and Man*' today beckons us for greater global cooperation and for more cooperative decision-making. "*There is not much time left for the planet to be saved*".

Is development sustainable? : Some relevant postulates

"Where there is no vision, people perish"

Is a well-known planning axiom. The evidence at our disposal clearly shows trends, which mark an increasingly stressed relationship between our national economies and the earth's ecosystems, which are taking a growing economic toll. Sustainable development calls for a radical transformation of the environment and argues that environmental problems need to be considered within the global economic system and that the degradation of the environment is not '*natural*', but an historical process linked to economic and political changes. In developing countries like ours, environmental management is no doubt assuming more importance as the contradictions of development—desertification, deforestation, and food insecurity are becoming more and more significant. Providing a vision of an environmentally sustainable economy, along with a road map to reach this goal is undoubtedly a big paradigmic shift , involving vital changes in the mindset of the population. Many thinkers have suggested some solutions. They are all either in the nature of concepts, perspectives or models. I can only cite a few.

(i) Eco-development within the carrying capacity of the Earth with *FIVE major OBJECTIVES*, which is a valid concept, but whose methodology has to be defined within each CONTEXT i.e. national and sub-national framework.

(ii) A systems approach to planning called "*Co-evolutionary approach*" in which Knowledge, Values, Resources,

Technology and Social Organization have been identified as the crucial sub-systems that would support one another. Each sub-system is related to all the others, but each is changing and affecting the evolution of the others. No sub-system will dominate another. They will all co-evolve to achieve sustainable development. This view has been expressed by Nogaard, who himself considers this as only a '*perspective*' and not really a model.

(iii) A model of planning for an "*Eco-economy*" *has been* advocated by Lester Brown, President of "*The Earth Institute*" in Washington. Brown has described how to restructure the global economy to make it compatible with the Earth's eco-system, so that economic progress can continue forever. In this new eco-economy visualized by him, wind energy will replace coal-mines, hydrogen-powered fuel cells will replace internal consumption engines and cities will be designed for people, and not for cars.

Such drastic changes can be brought about only through vigorous advocacy, appeals, exhortations and motivations, in which the role of each citizen of the earth is important. The efficacy of this approach has been demonstrated in China by President Mao, who made a clarion call for 'Greening the land' through his slogan "*go to Tachai and learn*". As the story goes, people went to Tachai and learnt some lessons in sustainable development.

Awareness building and advocacy are the two major functions of the Bhoovigyan Vikas Foundation. In this context, it is vigorously advocating the celebration of "*Earth-Day*", synchronizing with the equinoxes, when days and nights are equal. Another major advocacy is the building of open "*Museums of Earth, Man and Environment*". One such museum is already coming up in Raipur in the state of Chhattisgarh. Undoubtedly a search for a common direction or broad vision is necessary to tackle the challenges of population and environment.

In the end, Ladies and Gentlemen, I would like to place before you a developmental agenda, for the consideration of this College authorities. Please treat it as my earnest request. One is: please celebrate the Earth Day in your College on the day of the Equinox.

The BVF will give you all the necessary guidance and directions for celebrating it, as the "Thanks-giving Day" for Mother Earth. Our book on "*The Earth Day and its Significance*" is now under print. My second suggestion is that if you have enough land in your campus, create an "Open Air Geography Museum", carrying a specific message for "Saving our Planet". For both these innovations, I assure you of our cooperation. Friends, in this brief talk, I have attempted to outline some pathways to a sustainable future. The question still remains, "*which way do we want to go?*" That reminds me of a quotation from "*Alice in Wonderland*" by Lewis Carroll.

"*Would you tell me please, which way I ought to go from here?*" said Alice.

"*That depends a good deal on, where you want to get to.*" said the Cheshire Cat.

15

Towards Achieving Development, Empowerment and Social Justice

Introduction

The title of this conference reflects the complex and multi-dimensional nature of development. It underlines the fact that development is not just '*change*', but is related to some core values and ethic, which are indicated in the expressions 'empowerment' and 'social justice'. Amartya Sen has convincingly argued elsewhere, that these values and goals of development are essential to expand people's "capabilities", to achieve what they deem to be of 'value', in their societal circumstances. Thus, development is a value-loaded expression.

An extension of the conceptualization of development as an '*expansion of people's capabilities*', is also closely related to, what may be termed as 'contextuality in terms of space' i.e. its opportunities and constraints from a geographic perspective. The contextuality that I refer to here is the territorial setting and its natural resources along with its potentialities and constraints for development. The most effective instrumentality for assessing the spatial contextuality and to understand the factors that shape individual deprivations, needs and capability patterns, is through the close analysis of our '*micro-socio-spatial milieus*' and planning from the bottom. This can be

* Delivered in the M.S. Swaminathan Research Foundation, Chennai, 6-8-2005.

effectively accomplished only on the basis of a strategy of planning for viable spatial units in our rural areas, which can be "a cluster of villages"

Our Development learning Curve. In the more than fifty years of our development learning curve, we have equated development primarily with economic growth. This growth mania of our planners has taken different forms or 'avatars'. At least, I can count eight of them, characterized by limited perceptions and the consequent deprivations. These are:

(i)	Jobless growth	i.e. growth without employment opportunities
(ii)	Ruthless growth	i.e. growth that has aggravated the inequalities
(iii)	Futureless growth	i.e. growth that has inhibited the development of future generations
(iv)	Voiceless growth	i.e. non-participatory growth
(v)	Rootless growth	i.e. growth that has destroyed the cultural roots of our society
(vi)	Inequitable growth	i.e. growth without redistribution
(vii)	Unsustainable growth	i.e. growth which has been environmentally destructive
(viii)	Dependent growth	i.e. Growth without self-reliance

Century of the Small and Global Village

During this development era, some big developments have also been planned and executed. In recent times, these have evoked in some quarters, severe condemnations for bringing great disasters and negative consequences, along with a growing sense of disillusionment and even despair. Arundhati Roy's observation (1999) is significant in this context, though one may have to take it with some caution. She said "who knows what the twenty-first century has in store for us-the dismantling of the big bombs, big dams, big ideologies, big contradictions, big countries, big wars and big mistakes. Perhaps we may like this century to be the *Century of the Small*". Alvin Tofler, in his book on "The Third Wave" had envisioned a global village, which has now become a reality. That perhaps dictates our path of development. Our planning now should descend to the micro level, if development, empowerment and social justice should be operationalised effectively to tackle the problems of growth, poverty, unemployment, inequality and deprivation in a realistic manner.

Alternative Frameworks of Development

After experiencing our disillusionment with the neo-classical belief of the self-correcting nature of market mechanisms (trickle down process), some success stories have emerged in a few countries which throw up some refreshingly unique alternative frameworks to address the fundamental concerns of development, empowerment and social justice. Some examples are

- Comilla (Bangladesh)
- Saemal Undong (South Korea)
- People's Participation Programme (FAO)
- Agro-Politan Approach—Friedmann
- The Chinese Model
- Kundrakudi (TAD-MIX)
- Bio-village Paradigm (MSSRF)
- Jana Utthan Approach (BAIF))

Taking note of these developments, in my presentation, I propose to indicate an approach to micro-level planning with a number of the above objectives, which I am sure will supplement and enrich Prof. Swaminathan's latest vision for '*knowledge diffusion*' through his "*Mission 2007*".

The B.V.F. Approach—Planning for Sustainable Societies in Viable Rural Space

The Bhoovigyan Vikas Foundation's approach to the planning of more than six lakhs villages in the country, aims to group them into viable village cluster units for rural planning for development, empowerment and social justice. These village clusters will be designed as 'cohesive micro-level planning communities', which can be delineated by taking into account, their social, economic and spatial linkages and interrelationships, as well as the power structure of the community. These clusters, with a 'focal village' in each, will be linked in a hierarchy of levels, with at least one core economic activity, identified as the base for its development and also having scope for diversification of economic activities in the long run. The micro unit should also have a minimum population threshold, which would supply labour for the economic activities as well as a reasonable market for its products and services.

Development, Empowerment and Social Justice-Conceptual Underpinnings

I now set out my arguments for adopting this micro level approach for achieving development, empowerment and social justice. Initially, perhaps it is necessary to unwind or unlock some conceptual and philosophical cobwebs or strands about the three meaningful expressions–*Development, Empowerment and Social Justice*. To me, *development* is a spatial concept, with three interacting principles- *space, work and folk*, ingrained in it (Figure 15.1). Space implies the natural environment with its resource endowments; work implies activities pursued with knowledge (i.e. learning) skills and technology; folk means people with their culture, beliefs, customs and institutions

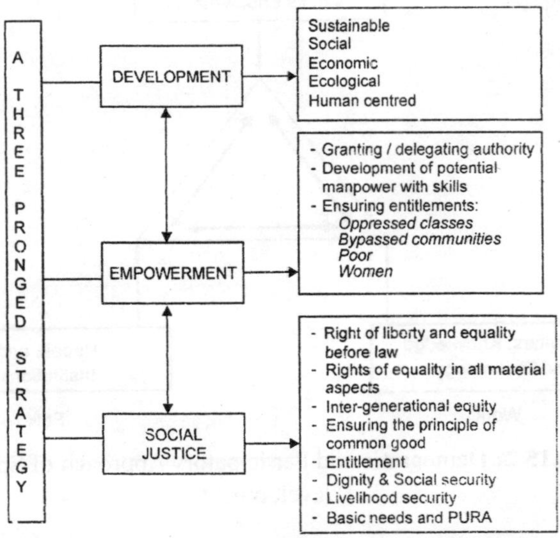

Fig.15.1: Achieving Development, Empowerment and Social Justice

Empowerment is an enabling measure, and a means to achieve enhanced socio-economic welfare. It means:

(i) Granting/delegating authority
(ii) Endowing the human resource with skills and abilities, and
(iii) Ensuring certain entitlements, which we call by the expression 'basic minimum needs' like food, fuel, shelter, sanitation and health.

The term *social justice* implies:

(i) The right of liberty and equality before law
(ii) Fairness in the distribution of benefits
(iii) Inter-generational equity in the consumption of natural resources, and
(iv) Ensuring the principle of common good.

The coverage and dimensions of development, empowerment and social justice are shown in Fig. 15.2.

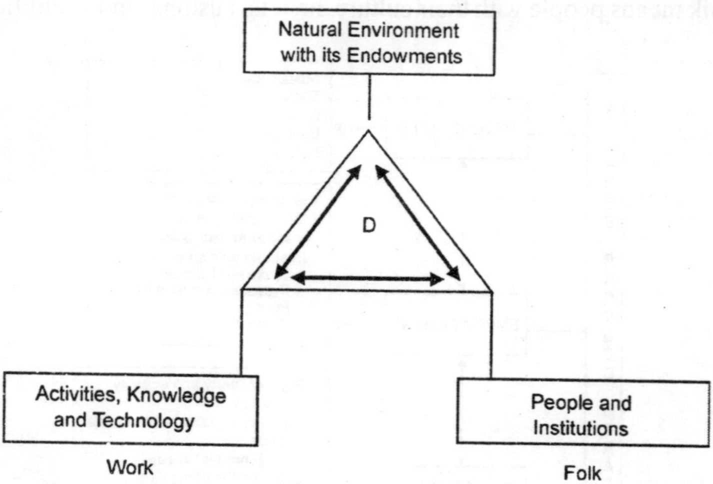

Fig.15.2: Democratic and Participatory Approach of Spatial Development

In order that the above conceptualisation can be translated into reality, we have to plan from below, so that we come into 'close grips' with capabilities and contextualities, to which I made a reference earlier. Such an approach requires appropriate methodologies. I shall explain the BVF approach for an Auto-kinetic Model of Development to lead us to this path.

A Multi-level modelling strategy-The Auto-Kinetic Model of Development; By auto-kinetic development, we mean a process, of Multi-Level modelling strategy through which the *autocentric* and *autodynamic forces* of development will be unleashed, which will release the inner urges, potentials and energies inherent in the local community. It is a process of engineering the overall development of productive forces, with the objective of better satisfying the basic livelihood and the material needs of the rural population, based as far as possible on a more intensive utilisation of local resources, by means of locally adapted and locally controllable, labour-intensive and small-scale technologies. Closely linked to this concept are the emancipatory as well as the socio-political and socio-cultural aspects of development, such as reformatory programmes, self-determination and self-direction, and the impulse for change coming through "capillary or trickle-up" effect and passing upward from the local, through the regional and national levels.

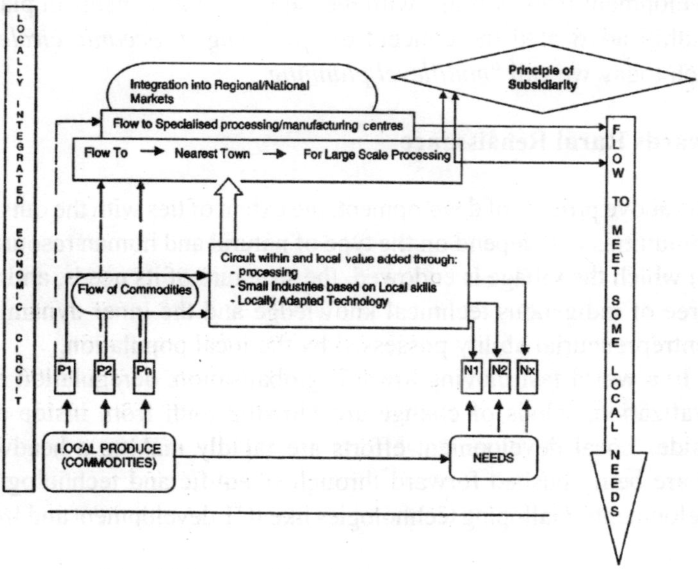

Fig. 15.3: Auto-kinetic Model of Development

In the auto-kinetic development approach, the basic objective of achieving the full-scale development of the natural resources and human skills available in the villages can be secured only by establishing "locally integrated economic circuits".

In this approach, the resource potential is analyzed primarily to see, where possibilities exist for improving the satisfaction of the local needs, with the assistance of locally adapted processing and small-scale technologies and by developing the functioning systems of circular flows, chain effects, and linkage effects i.e. forward and backward linkages.

The auto-kinetic development process rests on the *hierarchic principle of subsidiarity*. That is, we seek to establish processing/ manufacturing units at higher level only when the existing technologies and skills do not allow these to be performed in a satisfactory fashion and at a justifiable cost in the lower spatial levels. In other words, rural economy must be localized and diversified, so that nothing that is produced in the village goes outside of it in the raw form. As far as possible, it must be processed locally, by using the labour and skills of the local population. This is a variant of the concepts of "*Limited Spatial Closure*" and "*Inclusive Localism in Development*".

This is based on the Gandhian concept of "village swaraj" or 'development from within', with the capillary mechanisms in place. Gandhiji advocated the concept of "*planning in oceanic circles*", which today we call "*multilevel planning*".

Towards Rural Renaissance

In the above process of development, the extent of ties with the outside communities will depend on the type of natural and human resources with which the village is endowed, the structure of its needs, and the degree of indigenous technical knowledge and the inner dynamism or entrepreneurial ability possessed by the local population.

In a world fast moving towards globalisation, deregulation and privatization, winds of change are blowing both from inside and outside. Local development efforts are rapidly making a headway and are being pushed forward through scientific and technological developments. Galloping technologies like ICT development and fresh initiatives like the '*knowledge centre approach*' are making rapid strides. Time does not stand still. In this context, rural India must scale up on the principle of 'One Candle Lighting the Other' and graduate from pilot experiments in auto-kinetic development to a massive country-wide Rural Renaissance Movement.

Spatially-oriented disciplines like Geography and Agriculture sciences have a great role to play in bringing about this revolution. Lead institutions in the country like the I.I.M. and I.I.T. can play a critical role by bringing about this revolution.

VI
Decentralised Planning

16

Capacity Building for Strengthening Participatory Planning: Some Innovative Approaches

Introduction

This paper seeks to discuss some innovative approaches followed in action-oriented training for decentralized planning in two significant contexts viz: (a) an International Training Programme, focused on enhancing regional development planning capabilities in developing countries and (b) a Country-specific Training programme, aimed at operationalising decentralized planning at the district level. The former programme aimed at the training of a "critical mass" of regional planners in the developing countries and was experimented by the United Nations Centre for Regional Development (UNCRD) at Nagoya, Japan during 1972-79. The latter programme refers to an FAO/UN assisted project with Swiss funding in Nepal from 1983-90, which was primarily aimed at operationalsing the Decentralization Act of 1984 in the country and building up the capabilities for planning among the District and Central Government functionaries. In both the projects, the author played a crucial role, as a Consultant to the first experiment (i.e. UNCRD) and as Project Manager and Chief Technical Adviser to the second one (i.e. Nepal experiment). Both the experiments followed an *inductive* approach built around a planning exercise (as against only a deductive approach, which is being followed in most training programmes). As such, in both contexts they followed an intensely practical approach, with the planning methodology suited to the particular context, being evolved "in the field," without resorting to any intuitive and generalized formulations.

The Basic Principles

This approach is also referred to as the "Planning Exercise Oriented Training Approach" (PEOT). Such an approach is based on the principle of "learning by doing". The basic idea here is that training activities cannot be confined merely to problem identification and acquainting trainees with some sophisticated techniques. More important, trainees have to learn how to work as member of a planning team and formulate "implementable" development plans and to increase their capacity to manage development projects and programmes. This means that training will be closely linked with action, step by step. For this purpose, the team approach to training was advocated. The approach here was to train all the planners in the selected region/district as a "team", to the extent that they acquired a critical minimum of knowledge and skills, to enable them to formulate a development plan for the region/district, where they lived and worked. The main feature of the plan would be that it will be formulated by the local officials themselves and not by a group of external experts. The strategy is to first build up a core group-a team of trained planners in each region/district concerned. This is to be followed by the provision of other opportunities (i.e., through seminars, workshops, colloquia, etc.) for decision-makers, research personnel, and specialists to upgrade their knowledge and understanding of development planning.

The above basic principles were common to both the Nagoya and Nepal models. But in the operationalisation of the training programmes, there are some differences, which will become apparent later, when we discuss these models separately.

The Conceptual Framework for Training

Basic to evolving any approach to training is a sound conceptual framework. In the training context, I call this as the "Model of an instruction cycle". This instructional cycle relates to the issues of a learning-teaching process and the sequence in which they have to be organized, in order to facilitate easy learning and effective internalization of the knowledge and skills imparted during the training course. A model of an instructional cycle for decentralized planning at the district level is conceived in two phases. Its essential ingredients are set out below.

These are : (i) A first phase of training to promote among the trainees, a process of "divergent thinking" and (ii) A second phase to enable them to develop, what may be termed "convergent thinking". The first phase is a period during which the horizon of understanding of the trainees on development issues is sought to be widened, their short-sightedness or "blinkers" removed, and they acquire meta-disciplinary vision to enable them to become good and effective planners. This is a phase of long-duration training, during which the essential knowledge and skills are imparted and some "ancillary competencies" are developed, e.g. skills in gathering relevant information, in processing or analyzing the information and in assessing alternatives and more important, the 'social skills' that lead to attitudinal change. The class room training part consists of three interrelated activities viz. : (i) Seminars/Workshops conducted by the core trainers to impart the essential knowledge (concepts and methods); (ii) Special lectures by academics and specialists providing some holistic perceptions on some selected issues related to development planning; and (iii) Some lectures by practitioners in Government to provide reductionist/concrete/practical perspectives on planning for development. The knowledge and skills derived from class room lectures and exercises is further augmented through library readings, during which the participants study "recommended readings," selected for them by the training faculty. A third dimension of training relates to fieldwork, during which a field exercise is conducted by the participants under the supervision of the core trainers. A fourth dimension consists of presentation of selected case studies and survey or evaluation reports and the practice of some planning games. Problem-based discussions and group work may be deemed as a fifth dimension.

When these are systematically gone through, the trainees would have acquired considerable knowledge and skills and a process of intensive education becomes complete, leading to "divergent thinking". Then they get back to their jobs in the district.

During their stay in the districts, they are expected to apply some aspects of the knowledge and skills acquired by them in their day-to-day jobs. This phase of on-the-job application of the learning acquired by them during the training period depends much on the opportunities available in their work situation and the support of the superiors. This constitutes the first cycle of training. In my view, this first cycle, which enables the trainees to experiment with or put into practice some of the knowledge and skills acquired by them during their jobs would be incomplete without a second cycle.

The second phase, called 'Refresher Training', is a period during which the trainees: (a) acquire some new learning; (b) recall their past learning; (c) get their actions/experimentations on-the-job reviewed by the core trainers; and (d) generally reflect and interact with the trainers and other fellow-participants, which enables them to internalize and assimilate a good part of their learning and integrate the same with their prior knowledge. This helps them to conceptualize their experiences and leads to higher order perceptions. This, in turn, leads to innovation and creativity, which finds expression again in their day-to-day jobs, when they get back to their districts.

Thus the two phases of training described above constitute a complete instructional cycle (See Figure 16.1). In actual practice, the assumption of a "closed experiment" which is implied here may or may not obtain, as the trainees may be transferred from their jobs, which may or may not give them the same opportunities for application of their learning; or there may be other hindering factors preventing them from either applying their knowledge in their work situations or come again for a refresher programme, as envisaged here.

With the above conceptual background we may now consider the main features of the Nagoya and Nepal models of training.

The Nagoya Model

The UNCRD held its first International Training Programme, with the Bicol region in the Philippines as its "laboratory area". It was a 4 months training programme (February-June, 1974) with 26 trainees from 13 developing countries, consisting of mid-career government officials, directly concerned with comprehensive regional

in the region concerned (in relation to the national context) will be made, with the aim of improving the existing information network or proposing new information systems for regional planning in the subsequent phases. The activities in this phase will contribute to the designing of the contents of Phase II, which will fit the needs of the country and region concerned.

Phase II will provide basic training for the regional planning staff in the country concerned, with a curriculum designed to provide knowledge and skills tailored to the needs of the particular country and region. The team approach to training will be adopted. Each team will have five to ten members or perhaps more. The composition of each team will differ from one country to the other in terms of disciplines, sectors, and level of government representation. However, a team will be drawn mainly from a particular region with a regional development authority and will include some members coming from the National Planning Agency in charge of coordinating the planning activity at the regional level, as well as some members from the research and training institutions located in (or nearest to) the region concerned. The composition of the team, however, could be varied according to circumstances. These teams will form the core group for the on-the-job training activities.

The basic training course will provide an international inter-disciplinary experience. It will emphasize exchanging experiences in regional development and the team approach to learning. It will provide the basis for continuing the efforts of the trainees by keeping them in touch with each other and by keeping them informed of the latest thinking on regional development. In terms of content, the training course will expose the trainees to the full range of issues in planning for Comprehensive Regional Development. These are: (a) issues encountered in plan implementation, (b) national-regional-local coordination as well as inter-sectoral coordination of development activities and of the personnel involved, (c) issues faced in mobilizing resources for regional development and, (d) issues dealing with the multi-level political and cultural context of regional planning.

The planning team will work on the specific region in the country concerned. During the basic training course, its members will be taught on how to formulate a comprehensive regional development plan by means of a planning exercise.

After the basic training course is over, the teams will go to the selected region and will form the task forces for planning attached to the agency in charge of regional development. Phase III can now be started. Phase III will be an on-the-job training set of activities that will guide each task force in working out the details of the plan for the selected region. These details will cover projects and their interrelationships, problems and intra-regional disparities and ways to resolve them, area development plans (districts, municipalities, towns, cities and villages), budgeting procedures, reporting procedures, and information systems required for planning in the region. The task forces will work with all local government agencies concerned. Each task force, being composed mainly of members of these agencies, will operate in close collaboration with all the institutions mentioned above in order to bring about a coordinated total development effort. Each task force will learn to work within existing political and administrative realities. This will not bar it from thinking about a long-term management system for regional development.

In order to accomplish its work, each task force will have to be kept in close touch with the people and their representatives and with all government agencies through a series of workshops and individuals living and working in the region. These workshops will become a systematic effort to elicit the people's ideas, analyse them meaningfully, formulate development objectivities reflecting local needs, in order to select feasible and acceptable priority projects for implementation. The results of these workshops and consultations will be fitted into the regional planning framework. The task forces will be expected to learn how to conduct workshops effectively, in order to encourage popular participation in regional planning.

Towards the end of the third phase, after the plan for the comprehensive development of the region is completed, the task forces involved will assist in conducting a national training course, duration varying from eight to twelve weeks, for regional planners from other regions in the country. This national training course will use the planning experience in the region, where the task forces worked, and will study the completed final-draft of the first-cycle plan as a case. The task force members will be the teachers for this training course, assisted by consultants and other experts, whenever necessary. In this way, the planning experience that had been gained (which otherwise will be confined to only one of many regions) will be used to spark off more regional development activities and will be diffused widely in the country.

While the planning exercise was completed according to the time schedule, and the training programme as a whole was deemed a success in the sense, that it could accomplish what was envisaged during the training period, it cannot be so said about the post-training performance envisaged in the technical assistance model. As may be noted from the model, much of the initiative for the post-training follow-up lay with the trainees selected from the country, in which the case region is located. On account of the rather low-keyed follow-up performance that ensured (for several reasons, administrative and others), many of the activities that were envisaged in the regional model, could not materialize. Later, in an informal evaluation of the programme by UNCRD staff members, it was decided that the post-training follow-up should be institutionalized and not left to the spontaneity of the trainees from the country. Accordingly, in the next training programme organized in 1975 in Indonesia, a one and a half year post-training phase was also planned. UNCRD saw that one Adviser was stationed in the case study region during the period, who backstopped the activities of the trainees drawn from Indonesia by way of providing work guidelines and advisory services. Some specific work assignments were also planned during the on-the-job training phase.

Lessons from the Nagoya Model

In a dispassionate analysis of the Nagoya model, the following conclusions emerge:

1. Like the participant-observation technique in social science research, the PEOT provides an opportunity for the trainee to become an active participant in a live planning situation, enabling him to learn as well as to contribute to the process of planning and development.
2. The participant trainee not merely acquires a critical minimum knowledge and skills demanded of a regional

planner, but also learns how to effectively function and interact as member of an interdisciplinary planning term: shedding light without generating heat. The latter is a distinct behavioural and attitudinal gain that stands him in good stead in his professional career.

3. So far as the training institution is concerned, the PEOT is a highly demanding exercise. It needs a considerable lead time to complete the pre-training activities. It demands that a good deal of data collection, analysis and research must precede the training phase. If the impact is seriously desired, then it is necessary also to plan for the post-training phase in a meticulous manner by making such institutional arrangements as necessary.
4. So far as the time duration is concerned, the PEOT needs a fairly long period of time. In the UNCRD experience, about 6 months were required for the training phase alone, as it entailed field work, visits to various offices and considerable dialogue, both with officials as well as the people, to understand the various facts of the development problem.
5. The pre-training and post-phase training activities are equally important and they demand at least 3 to 4 times the duration of the training phase. When the training period is of long duration, and it is meant for senior and middle level personnel, many governments find it difficult to release such personnel for long periods. This is a practical constraint that has to be kept in view, while organizing such programmes.
6. In terms of cost also, PEOT is an approach which demands considerable sums of money. First, there are the pre-training costs to be met. Secondly, during the training phase, money has to be provided for field work and travel.
7. The PEOT approach, it must be understood, is not merely exercise-oriented, but also trainee-centred. As planning is a multi-level and multi-sectoral activity, the composition of the planning team must have a multi-disciplinary character, so that the various aspects of planning will receive proper attention. In this context, a good deal of care is necessary in regard to the selection trainees, as ultimately the planning team should be representative of the numerous disciplines.

8. In terms of its impact, however, the PEOT approach is to be highly commended. Through a judicious combination of lectures, discussions, field work and the planning exercise, it would be possible for the trainees to learn more here than through any other method.
9. As the UNCRD experience revealed, the impact of the PEOT approach is especially great in a country-specific situation, as it is directly relevant to the path of development pursued in the country and enables the trainees to understand the problems and prospects inherent in the development process operating in this country.

The FAO/UN Nepal Model

The FAO/UN assisted the Government of Nepal with technical assistance in developing planning capabilities during 1978-90 in two phases. During the first phase (1978-83), the FAO assisted the country in capacitation, centred on project approach with emphasis on people's participation. A Training Section was established in an already existing institution called the "Agricultural Project Services Centre" (APROSC) in Kathmandu and trainers were recruited, who were trained in Project Formulation techniques and in Monitoring and Evaluation techniques. During the second phase (1983-98), the focus of training shifted to Decentralised Planning.

During this phase, the training needs for decentralized planning were assessed and six categories of target groups were identified.

(i) District Level Officers
(ii) Office Assistants
(iii) Village Panchayat Secretaries
(iv) District Panchayat Members
(v) Village Chairman/Vice-Chairman
(vi) Ward Chairman and Ward Members

Later, a "*training-cum-technical assistance cycle*" was initiated in one of the districts of Nepal viz. Tanahun district in the Western Development Region. With the assistance of all district officials, a plan for the district was prepared as an on-the-job training exercise, with the FAO consultants backstopping the exercise with technical guidance and assistance.

This experience, besides providing training services and helping one district to prepare a plan, also enabled the APROSC Training Section (APROSC-TS) to prepare a first draft of training materials. These needed considerable refinement and systematization before they could be turned into a comprehensive Training Manual. In the meantime, a number of changes took place in Nepal during the operationalization of the Decentralization Act and its bye-laws. There were also new policy initiatives introduced by HMG/N, like the emphasis on basic needs etc. In this context, it was realized that it was necessary to have a fresh look at the training materials available, fill up their gaps, introduce new elements and turn them into a systematic manual, which can be used by all training institutions in the country. The finalization of theTraining Manual and the running of training programmes for the district level functionaries based on the manual were the accomplishments during the third phase (1988-90).

A modular approach was followed in the preparation of the manual, and the whole content of training was presented in eight modules. The titles of the eight modules were as follows.

1. Understanding Development
2. Decentralization and the Planning Process in Nepal.
3. District Planning: An Analytical Process
4. Techniques and Tools for District Planning
5. District Plan Formulation.
6. Implementation and Management of District Plans.
7. Popular Participation
8. Development Support Communication for District Development.

The eight modules of the Manual have been structured into 67 subject areas (lessons or discussion sessions) and incorporate 16 exercises and 3 case studies, besides one participatory planning game. This is intended for a 4 to 6 week's training course.

What is unique about the training manual is that it has emerged from the live situation of an action-planning-cum-training exercise. Such an exercise enabled the training institution to render the teaching materials as close to realities as possible. This also helped in the greater impact of training in the on-the-job performance of the trainees.

Secondly, the experience showed that despite the existence of a manual, the trainers cannot rest on their arm chairs, but need to continually engage themselves in studies, first for updating the manual in terms of new procedures, rules and regulations introduced by the government from to time, and secondly to undertake area-specific case studies to illustrate the use of specific methods, tools and techniques for district planning. This means that the training professionals must eschew 'ivory towers' and "get their hands dirty", by frequently going to the field and conducting studies. Thus the preparation of teaching materials is a continuous activity and cannot be terminated with the preparation of training manual. Thus training is to be viewed as a *Research-çum-training activity*. Action research is an important component here, as it is only through action research that problems confronting decentralized planning could be perceived and innovative solutions found.

The training programmes which were run by the institution followed, what is called a "Repeat-Contact-Method" or "a Sandwich pattern" of training. Thus training was not conceived as one-shot operation.

In this type of training, the trainees, after gaining an initial exposure to some knowledge and skills went back to their jobs in the district for about a year, during which they conducted some exercises in their work places. Then they came back to the training institution for a refresher phase, during which their work was reviewed.

The most interesting aspect of the FAO Training Model was the manner in which the follow-up phase was pursued. During the course of the training, the trainees were encouraged to identify an aspect of the training curriculum, which were most important from the point of view of their work-situation. After the training was over and when they were working in their offices, they were asked to apply the knowledge gained in their work situation to this perceived aspect. This required the support of their superiors. The training institution wrote to their superiors calling their attention to the aspect or problem identified by the trainee and requesting them to lend their support in carrying out this exercise. During this period, the trainers also visited in their work-places and provided them such guidance or technical support as necessary. In this manner, great care was taken to increase the impact of the training.

It is often said that in any radical approach to training the participants must be to enable to decide the content of the curriculum themselves. It may be noted that the "Follow-up Method" practiced by the FAO model came somewhat close to this "demanded approach" to training.

Adaptation of the Models to the Capacitation Approach in our Present Context

Both the technical assistance model (with its implication of some external intervention) and the 'repeat'—contact method (sandwich type of training with its implication of an intensive follow-up phase) are quite relevant in our present Indian context. Our major constraints now are:

(i) Scarcity of trainers
(ii) Scarcity of training institutions

In the above context, one feasible solution could be for the National Institute of Rural Development (NIRD) to tackle the training problem in association with the State Institute of Rural Development (SIRD) in the states in a highly organized and systematic manner as follows:

The NIRD, with its team of trained personnel, will organize the training of trainers, all drawn from the SIRD's. It will be in the nature of 'ACTION TRAINING' with a chosen district, as its laboratory area. During this training programme, the trainees will prepare a village plan, a block plan and a district plan. Through this action programme, they will learn all the essential analyses for planning and the various procedures for project formulation and their integration. The trainees from the SIRD's will, after returning to their states, in turn, conduct similar training programmes, drawing the trainees from the districts in their states and adopting one of the districts for the training exercise. In this way, one lamp will light the other and the training exercise will go on.

In the exercises on plan preparation, owing to time constraints, only the major steps and analyses involved in planning could be covered. Broadly, these may include:

(i) Date and information collection and processing (Participatory appıaisal techniques)
(ii) Analyses needed for Macro-framework building (i.e., goals/ objectives setting: strategy formulation etc.)
(iii) Analyses needed for plan formulation viz.-
- Area Analysis
- Analyses for project identification and formulation
- Analyses for formulation and integration of development proposals (integration of rural and urban plans)
- Analysis for implementation planning (Monitoring and Evaluation techniques)

The NIRD, after completing the course of training will prepare a detailed training manual, setting out the readings, the exercises etc. and provide detailed guidelines for decentralised planning. In this exercise, the NIRD will have to assume a certain pattern of devolution of functions, which may be considered "ideal". When applied to any state, it may have to be modified, as necessary, to the state situation.

The task seems difficult and challenging. But there are no options here but to go ahead with some normative assumptions and yet systematic procedures. In the "transition stage", where we are now, an "incremental strategy" to capacitation is the only feasible solution. Perfection may come, when each state government has been able to set up adequate number of training institutions with qualified and trained staff. Even during the transitional stage, SIRD's have to make up their short comings by partly engaging academic personnel in universities and colleges and highly qualified retired personnel, as may be available in the area.

17

From Top-Down Planning to Decentralised Regional and Local Development in India-Vision and Reality: Challenges and Perspectives

The evolution of development planning in India spanning over half a century is a fascinating story. The spatial dynamics of change here—from top-down planning to decentralised regional (state) and local development—is marked by struggles and challenges, in which the years 1969 (the commencement of the Fourth Five Year Plan) and 1993 (the Legislation of Constitutional Amendments) stand out as significant milestones marking the first and second stages of decentralisation, respectively. The progression from centralized planning to regional and local autonomy in planning and decision-making, with its undertones of centre-state relations, is an on-going process of multilevel participatory planning. It is new in its style, stance and substance, and is yet to be perfected, both in its planning and governance dimensions. Several initiatives have been made by the government towards decentralisation since Independence, the latest being the innovation for according constitutional status to panchayats. While enfranchisement and some degree of empowerment at the local level are the distinct gains, the panchayats are not yet functioning as units of self-government.

---

* Still an ethical code of functioning with a moral code of conduct is a far cry. Indian Social Service Review, 2-2-2000, Sage Publications, New Delhi, Thousand Oaks, London.

Introduction[1]

This paper sets out some reflections on the history of development planning in India with sub-national (regional) and local development as its major focus. In essence, it is the story of the grand vision that prompted rural spatial planning and development in India and the reality that finally asserted itself during the burgeoning of the development process. The author has woven into this tapestry an insider's knowledge and outsider's perception, on the varied aspects of sub-national development planning in India. An analysis in retrospect, such as the one attempted here, has its own relevance. It offers some insights into what happened, and why and how it happened. Further, it also prompts one to reflect on alternative development strategies that could, perhaps, have been more helpful. In any case, it constitutes an essential dimension of inquiry while thinking about our future, as we have entered a new century and millennium, and must draw some lessons from the past.

The Early Beginnings: Centralised Planning[2]

India attained Independence in 1947, and the new Nation began, in the 1950s, to construct an economically strong and socially just society. What should be the model of development was a major question. Our first Prime Minister was fascinated by the Soviet model of centralised economic planning, and he installed a version of the Russian Gosplan organisation in our country, by creating a 'think-tank'—in the form of the National Planning Commission—to carry out the task of planning. The vision was noble and the mood optimistic. Since development was a serious and passionate business, there were heated arguments, debates, and agreements and disagreements among the intellectuals on various pertinent issues regarding planning and development.

In the 1960s, administrative reforms and the reorganization of states were important subjects of debate. Even after the government decided to adopt the model of linguistic states, there were still some lingering doubts about the validity of this criterion, as suitable areal units for planning and development. Fond hopes of establishing a new spatial order in the form of 'economic regions' persisted in some quarters. Many studies were initiated in this context. Rational economic planning, rather than cultural differentiation, and the politics associated with it, was the main concern of this approach, which led to vigorous advocacy of *resource-based regionalization,* as a tool for planning purposes.[3]

In this context, inter-and intra-regional differentials in resource endowments, interlinked distributional patterns of resources, settlement patterns, commodity flows and other regional phenomena, including socio-cultural dimensions, came to be perceived and analysed as important region-forming factors. A number of contributions not only examined the concept of regionalization, but also provided concrete systems of alternative 'economic regions' for the country (Learmonth and Bhat 1962; Misra *et al.* 1974; Nath, 1965; Prakasa Rao and Bhat 1964; Sen Gupta and Galina Sadasyuk, 1961). Most of these studies were conducted by geographers and in terms of techniques, they experimented with various cartographic analyses, combined with simple statistical approach to regionalization. They considered the spatial patterns of natural economic resource configurations, the existing level of economic, social and physical developments, and the potential for future development, and sought to combine local administrative units (districts) into meaningful composite regions. Some studies were influenced by the Russian model of 'territorial production complexes' (Sen Gupta and Galina Sadasyuk, 1961). Maximum distinctiveness, minimum inter-regional differences, economic specialisation of areas, community of interest, economic viability and ecological balance were some of the guiding principles or criteria in the approaches to regionalization followed in these studies. Some studies also considered, besides the differences and similarities of areas in resource endowments, the interaction of people and economies. (Berry 1966). International debates in several world fora (like the International Geographical Congress at Rio de Janeiro (1956) and in Stockholm) also promoted studies on the regionalization. During the Third Five Year Plan period, the Government of India's concern centred on the development of the backward areas which were marked by growing regional disparities in development in the country and the need for evolving regional policies in this context.

As these ideas were in circulation, the Town and Country Planning

Organisation (TCPO), an agency of the Central Government, sought to operationalise a plan scheme of *'Inter-state Regional Planning'*, with its thrust on formulating appropriate regional policies, and introducing a 'regional factor' in economic development. It used the studies on economic regionalisation to identify inter-state (groups of states) regions, that would facilitate economic integration.[4]

In retrospect, the notion of 'inter-state regions', at a time when the planning process had not yet been effectively decentralised to the state level, was a milestone concept, seeking to introduce a new geographical scale in planning, with its set of 'regional policies' at the meso level, for supporting a general policy of national economic development. It was this concept of regional policies that ultimately triggered off the thinking on rectifying regional imbalances in the country and for taking some positive steps in this direction. This led to the formulation of certain programmes in the five year plans, which sought, to bring into the main-stream of development, those bypassed and other marginal regions, which had not participated fully in growth, which had unused or underused resources, and which suffered from some economic, social or technological disadvantage, causing problems in development.

Southeast Resource Regional Planning: An Unfinished Agenda[5]

As a first step towards the objective of progressively achieving a balanced form of regional development in the country, planning was undertaken for one major resource region-the 'coal-steel belt of India'. This region-called the 'South-East Resource Region (SERR)-consisted of parts of five states, that is, West Bengal, Bihar, Orissa, Madhya Pradesh and Uttar Pradesh. It was conceived as a collaborative model of planning in a 'partnership approach', with the centre and the concerned states collaborating in the preparation of a macro-regional plan, and the TCPO acting as its technical secretariat. It was a unique effort, '*a work of some awesome earnestness*', providing an excellent illustration of collective decision-making in the federal context, with the participating states joining the venture in a spirit of co-operation and collaboration.

In spite of its intrinsic merits, the inter-state planning exercise failed to take roots. There were various reasons for this failure, including: (a) the inability of the states to carry forward the exercise to its logical conclusion towards effective sub-regional and local-level planning; (b) the lack of political will in some states to undertake such comprehensive exercise; (c) the introduction by the centre, of certain vital changes in the mode of channelling plan assistance to the states; and (d) the formulation of some innovative central and centrally sponsored plan schemes by the centre as an alternative method of bringing about balanced regional development in the country.

While the year 1969 marked the beginning of a new phase of planning in India, it was so, in the global context too. It was during this year, that Dr. Dudley Seers, a former director of the Institute of Development Studies, Sussex (UK), published his seminal paper on "The Meaning of Development (Seers 1969, 1977). Dr. Seers characterised the 'trickle-down theory' of development as a mere figment of imagination-'a web of fantasy', as he put it. He questioned the received doctrines of economic growth and advanced new concepts. Development did not merely comprise economic growth or modernization. Of far more importance to third world countries was the problem of reducing the poverty level among the masses. In this context, the provision of employment and of 'basic' needs to target groups, and ensuring better income distribution and quality of life to the people were considered as the priority development issues. In the wake of this recognition, a succession of far-reaching ideas about development emerged during the 1980s and 1990s. They include several issues of great relevance, such as achieving sustainable development, gender equity, decentralisation, devolution and democracy, human development and adopting self-reliant approaches to development through local self-governing institutions and community-based organisations. Events pertaining to rural development planning in India reveal a similar sequence of thinking and development.[6]

From the Centre to States: The First Stage of Decentralisation: The Fourth Five Year Plan was a 'watershed' in India's planning effort and brought about a major shift of the planning process from the Centre to the states. This may be seen as the first stage in decentralisation. The centre took note of the evils inherent in following a prescribed schematic pattern of plan assistance and devised new procedures for the allocation of central assistance to the states as block grants and block loans by means of a formula, giving weightage to varying kinds of backwardness. This provided the freedom to the states to plan for their territories according to their needs and priorities. Explaining this departure, the Fourth Five Year Plan observed as follows:[7]

"In order to simplify the procedure for release of Central assistance, to avoid adoption of standard schemes unsuited to local conditions and needs, as well as to ensure equity among States in regard to the grant assistance for the Plan, it has been decided that in future, there will be no schematic patterns of assistance. Central assistance will not be related to any specific scheme or programme under the State Plans, but would be given to the States, through block grants and block loans. Each State will get a fixed proportion (30%) of Central assistance in the form of grant and the balance (70%) by way of loans. In order to ensure that the overall priorities of the plan are adhered to, outlays under certain heads or subheads of development and specified schemes will, however, be earmarked and will not be diverted to other heads of development (GOI 1969-74: 55)."

The Fourth Five Year Plan introduced a number of central and centrally sponsored schemes, intended as a 'balancing factor' to the state plans, to ensure that national objectives and priorities were preserved. The task of defining inter-regional policies was left to the sectoral wings and agencies of the Central ministries (for example, the Indian Council of Agricultural Research [ICAR] and the Council for Scientific and Industrial Research, [CSIR]). All these should be seen as major changes in the revolution of the planning system in the country.

The Fourth Plan also heralded the emergence of a number of target-oriented interventions-multiple alternate paradigms-to alleviate poverty, unemployment and backwardness, by adopting a selective development strategy and specific programmes. These programmes, called 'Special Group and Area Specific Programmes', commenced in the 1970s, and proliferated during the 1980s. Some of them are still continuing under different names. While formulating these new approaches, the centre innovated with new patterns of sharing finances with the State Governments. Two approaches are worth noting. One is the approach followed in the planning adopted for the tribal and hilly areas and the backward classes in society, known as the 'sub-plan approach'. A sub-plan is a disaggregated plan for an area within the state. It takes into account the financial resources that will flow into the area from the regular state plan funds, and the additional funds that the centre proposes to pump in to accelerate the development of the area. For this total funding, an internally consistent plan, with appropriate strategies and priorities, will be worked out. Thus, the sub-plan approach approximates to a typical area development approach. The second financing pattern experimented with by the centre is what has been known as an 'additive or supplemental' approach to finance specific schemes, which could not be funded adequately by State Governments and needed some additional supplementation from the centre. By the end of the Fifth Plan, the differentiated Sub-Plan had a wide coverage in the country. They were all meant as 'backward area development programmes' and were informed by different strategies and thrusts.[8]

Closing the Regional Gap: Theory and Practice; A distinct fallout of the exercises in 'regionalisation' and of planning for one 'inter-state region' on a pilot basis, was the awareness that grew among our policy-planners that a '*country is its regions*' and that regional development policies are indispensable for supporting a general policy of economic development. In particular, the centre became concerned about the growing regional imbalances in development, among and within states, and launched some initiatives to ensure that the benefits of development spread, as early as possible, among the different regions, in keeping with the national objective of economic growth with social justice.[9]

Two parallel lines of thought promoted this concern. The first was an imperative to counteract the centripetal forces inherent in economic growth, which had led to acute problems in some metropolitan cities like Delhi, Bombay and Calcutta. The second was the perception of some negative factors retarding spatial development, which had placed some regions at a disadvantage in relation to other regions in the country. Thus, the focus shifted to the problem of inter-regional disparities in development.

This became a subject of intensive research among social scientists, particularly during the period 1960 to 1975. Several scholars sought to portray the levels of development in the country by employing state-level, regional or district-level aggregations of selective indicators, and using various techniques to assess the level of development (Mathur 1978; Mitra 1961; Schwartzberg 1962, Sundaram 1982; Sundaram and Prakasa Rao 1971). The Central and State Governments also constituted some committees to examine the problem of backward areas. The committees included the *National Committee on the Development of Backward Areas,* 1978, known as the '*Sivaraman Committee*'; the *I.G. Patel Committee in Gujarat,* 1984; and the *Dandekar Fact Finding Committee on Regional Imbalances in Maharashtra,* in 1984. These committee reports were the precursors of the numerous 'Special Group and Area Specific Programmes', that have blossomed since the Fourth Five Year Plan (1969-74) in our plan programmes. Despite the implementation of the various policies and programmes aimed at the amelioration of economic backwardness over a fairly long period of 25 years or so, the problem of backward areas remains an intractable one. A comparison of the spatial structure of backwardness in the country between the 1979s and 1990s is afforded by two studies (Moni 1999; Sundaram and Prakasa Rao 1971) which have used identical techniques-*the principal components analysis*-and have delineated the constituents of 'underdeveloped India. See Maps 1 and 2, particularly the areas covered under the categories 'low and very low'.) The maps show that notwithstanding the changes that have occurred in absolute and incremental development over a period of about three development decades, the 'hard core areas of backwardness' remain the same. This 'hard core' covers a vast stretch of eastern, central and middle south India, not spread contiguously in a single block, but in an interspersed pattern. Within this hard core area, small areas stand out as 'islands' around some urban nodes, revealing a 'spotty' kind of relatively higher development that has not spread its effects in the surrounding rural areas. When studied in conjunction with the physical and agro-ecological patterns of development, the 'core areas of backwardness' or 'the problem areas' lie in certain well-defined agro-ecosystems of the country, that is, the irrigated, arid and rain-fed areas; the hill and mountain systems; and some parts of coastal areas.[10]

Thus, the geographical configuration of 'underdeveloped India', viewed from a policy angle, is not a single 'problem region', but lies scattered in diverse regions with markedly different natural resource endowments and socio-economic environments. In terms of its diversity, 'underdeveloped India' appears to be as diverse as the subcontinent itself (Sundaram 1982).[11]

If a taxonomic breakdown of underdeveloped areas can be attempted, they fall into five fairly compact regions, each with its own complex set of symptoms and causes, and perhaps even remedies. These are: (a) the north-eastern region of India; (b) the tribal belt in east-central India; (c) eastern UP and north Bihar; (d) the Bundelkhand region of UP and Madhya Pradesh; and (e) the ecologically unbalanced areas in the country with special problems, that is, drought-prone areas, desert areas, ravine areas, flood-prone areas and hill areas.

The Planning Commission studies indicated that economic backwardness in the country was due to three major causes (a) past historical neglect, leading to the typical 'bypassed areas' in development; (b) some adverse factor endowments, such as adverse climate, difficult terrain conditions, poor soil or lack of surface water; and (c) social backwardness, especially in areas inhabited by tribals, marginalised groups and oppressed communities, who have been subjected to various forms of economic exploitation, social discrimination and political isolation. The diagnosis revealed that in terms of concrete policies, plans and programmes, the first type of regions needed 'accelerated development' tailored to their specific historical contexts and resources endowments. That is to say, they generally needed more of the same forces of change as the more successful regions e.g. education, technological change, capital accumulation and the demonstration effect that works through the contact with other groups. The second type of regions needed rapid transformation through the contact with other groups. The second type of regions also needed rapid transformation through the application of modern science and technology. The third type of backward areas needed sympathetic treatment by creating countervailing forces of adequate dimension which could enable the inhabitants of these areas to retain their social ethos and to obtain a reasonable share in the fruits of development. This policy analysis revealed that if conscious efforts could be made to reverse the growth trends in this manner, the backward regions could be 'lifted' to the level of development achieved by more prosperous regions.[12]

Some Theoretical Underpinnings

At this stage, a brief diversion on some theoretical aspects of the backward area development problem would be interesting. Studies on backward areas in several developing countries in Asia and Africa have revealed that the 'regional gap' in these countries could be closed only through a planned incremental strategy of sustained and systematic effort (Sundaram 1982). The critical components of such a strategy would include:

- Adopting a typological approach to impart greater area specificity to all programme ingredients:
- Initiating a transition growth process to identify a dynamic policy programme package and to bring about a proper sequencing of the development process; and
- Exploiting the comparative advantage theory for suitably establishing appropriate 'sectoral' and 'spatial' leads in development.

In terms of programmatic interventions, the backward area development strategy must be characterized by (a) selectivity; (b) specificity or focus; and (c) dynamism and flexibility. Operationally, what is implied here is the need to make a deep thrust into an identified critical problem situation of a particular backward area through selective programmatic interventions, thus initially cracking the 'hard crust of backwardness' and breaking the key barriers to development (Figure 17.1). Thereafter, the development strategy should add other complementary investments, thus generally enlarging the scope and content of development interventions. This is really a problem of 'planning for transitional growth'-to plan as well as possible, for a situation of continuous rapid transition. During the transition, the economy and society of the backward area would move through some radical changes, resembling a process of evolution through time. During this phase of sequential change, the economy and society of the backward area would not only be growing in a quantitative sense, but also its basic rules of growth would be gradually modified. Undoubtedly, in the different types of backward areas, the patterns of transition would differ. Thus, it is clear that the backward area problem cannot be straightjacketed into one set of planning rules. The developments initiated in this manner are then expected to expand, through trickle-down and spread effects, as well as through multiplier effects, thus increasing their spatial coverage and 'saturating' the area. This implies progression from the particular to the universal, from a part to the whole and from selectivity to comprehensiveness. But such progression is highly hypothetical. In any case, the progression will not be along a straight line. In real life situations, no simple rules of progression are possible. This is an accepted fact.[13]

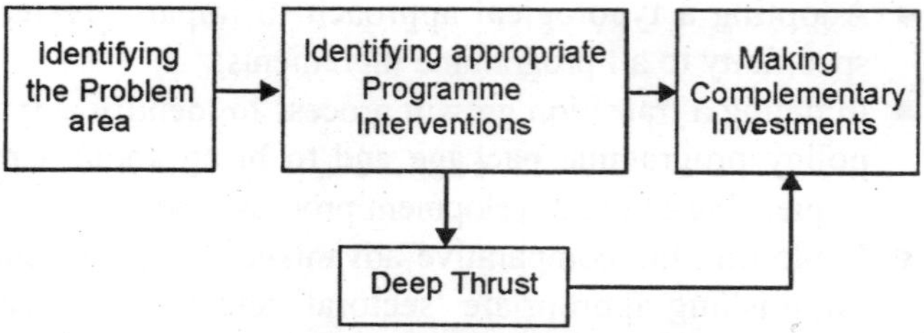

Fig. 17.1: The Backward Area Development Strategy.

If the above theory is any guide to the backward area development strategy, then having recognized the different typological development of backwardness in the country, developments should be carefully steered as a 'transition growth process', by identifying different policy and programme packages for each type of backward area. This should be informed by the comparative advantage principle for establishing appropriate sectoral and spatial leads in development and an 'incremental approach' for the allocation of development funds. This, however, did not happen with the Indian experience. Continuities in policies were consistently marred and, inevitably, the progressive acceleration of the development process in backward areas was sacrificed somewhere midway. Some components of the backward areas programme, like the 'Drought-Prone Areas Programme', the 'Tribal Development Programme', and the 'Small Farmers' Development Programme' have already been phased out and incorporated into the integrated Rural Development Programme. If we take stock of the numerous target group and target area interventions, in the nature of special programmes aiming at the removal of backwardness, poverty and unemployment in this country, that have proliferated since the Fourth Plan, the number is really amazing. Each change in political regime has spawned its own pet schemes, with different patterns of assistance, giving rise to a multiplicity and pluralism factor in development, with its attendant problems of integration and co-ordination in implementation.[14]

One of our former Finance Ministers, P. Chidambaram, has recently observed that ' these programmes are too many, lack focus, have multiple objectives, have been poorly designed with sub-critical investments and often overlap' (Chidambaram 1999). The lack of consistency in the approach and continuity of programmes also seriously marred the development of backward areas, leading to sub-optimal results. Further, during the implementation of the backward area programmes, no serious efforts were taken either to internalise the development process or to plug the leakages of various kinds and magnitude, with the result that they made little impact on the developments of areas or humans. A number of studies and analyses in underdeveloped economies have brought out the point that it is the leakages as well as the dependency structures that constitute the real reasons for backwardness. In sum, the Indian experiment on the development of backward areas was a veritable 'muddling through'[15] and a policy failure.

The Need for a Multilevel System of Planning

The Planning Commission was not unaware of the perplexities and dilemmas associated with backward area planning and the disjunction between the concepts and the reality. It was realised that while the planning process in India had succeeded in building up a network of relationships, comprising the centre, the states, the local bodies and the private sector, through a variety of devices, (financial, administrative and advisory), it still suffered from a number of deficiencies. Two deficiencies, in particular, were discernible as being responsible for rendering the plans somewhat inadequate, in terms of formulation and implementation. First of all, the flow of information between the various decision-making agencies involved was, generally speaking, very slow and quite inadequate. Second, the two principal actors in planning, the Centre and the states, were not moving in unison to achieve the objectives and priorities laid down in the plan. Also, the procedures employed by the Planning Commission to reach agreement on planning issues, which were a mixture of formal and non-formal devices, had not, however, succeeded in imparting the needed degree of rationality into the plan-making process (Chakravarty 1969). To overcome all these problems, the Planning Commission took a policy decision to the effect that the planning process in India should be viewed essentially as a multilevel operation that would seek to reconcile the territorial distribution of plan resources, while giving adequate scope to the state plans to emerge in accordance with their own perceptions of needs and priorities, It became essential to devise a system of information flows and delegation of responsibilities, coupled with suitable provision on the financial side. Multilevel planning, with its two-way planning process, became the new mantra and was recognised as a more helpful approach than the rather *ad hoc* procedures so far.[16]

Towards Decentralised Planning in a Two-Tier Federalism

Gandhiji used the expression 'Planning in Oceanic Circles' for the jargon 'Multilevel Planning' to describe the grass roots planning of his dream, with the Indian village as the basic societal unit, having maximum autonomy and maximum interdependence. One of the basic principles of multilevel planning, viz. the 'subsidiarity principle' or the principle of functional decentralisation, was described by him as the principle of 'swaraj'. This implied that 'what the village or village panchayat can do must be done in the village itself' (Gandhi 1947). It was a grand vision projected by Gandhiji during the pre-Independence era.

However, owing to a difference in views among the senior Congress leaders of those times, the Gandhian agenda of self-reliant village republics was ultimately given up in favour of a three-tier system of democratic institutions, called the 'Panchayati Raj Institutions (PRIs), built upon the dynamics of development ushered in by the successive five year plans since 1951. This followed the famous recommendations for democratic decentralisation by the Balwantrai Mehta Study Team in 1958 (GoI 1957). The PRIs, however became mere local-level executive agencies for implementing different plan projects, and certain occasional non-development schemes (census, elections, disaster relief, and the like). While their 'agency functions became pronounced, their democratic mainsprings were ignored, and they did not blossom into 'units of self-government' (Mathur 1995). By and large, they worked as the bureaucratically-controlled, state-funded delivery arms of the government, with the semblance of a democratic set-up. They passed through a phase of stagnation in 1965-69, and ultimately of decline in 1969-77. A point that must be emphasised in this context is that even at their peak in the early 1960s, they gave no meaningful slant to local-level planning. All the time, the Central Government was pushing and prodding the states through Expert Group Reports, Guidelines for Decentralised Planning and Central Assistance Schemes for building up state and district planning machineries etc. Despite all these measures, the commitment to local-level planning was tenuous and uneven among the states, and, on the whole, lackluster in performance.[17]

The Historic Change

The turnaround came with the enactment of three historic central legislations which came into effect from April 1993. These have sought to ensure the establishment of local self-government institutions throughout the country and have ushered in a new era of decentralisation in India. These three central acts are:

- The Constitution's 73rd Amendment Act, 1992
- The Constitution's 74th Amendment Act, 1992
- Provision of the Panchayats (Extension to the Scheduled Areas) Act, 1996.

They have ushered in a change in the 'basic structure' of the Indian Constitution, by recognizing the entities below the state level as constitutional bodies, and introducing a third stratum of local level (district) governance in India's political system.

Thus, the year 1993 is the cut-off point in the context of the evolution of local-level planning in India. For a meaningful analysis of sub-national local development in planning therefore, we should distinguish between two phases of development in the Indian experience in local planning: (i) a pre-1993 phase; and (ii) a post-1993 phase.

The Pre-1993 Phase Scenario[18]

Since the commencement of planning in India 1951, several initiatives have been taken by the government towards decentralised planning. The decentralisation policy adopted, however, has placed different emphasis at different times, with the result that planning and development at the sub-national levels have followed different impulses and taken several routes. (Vyas *et al.* 1985). As we look back in retrospect at the various policy shifts that have taken place, we may distinguish at least five different phases of change that have left their varying imprints on local-level planning and development. Table 17.1 seeks to capture these changes.

Table 17.1: Decentralised Rural Development: Different Phases

Phase	*Period*	*Major Changes*
I	1950-60	The transition from a law and order administrative system to a welfare and development-oriented system. The community development phase.
II	1960-70	The Panchayati raj phase.
III	1970-80	The special area development programmes phase. The block-level planning phase.
IV	1980-93	The district planning phase. Emphasis on poverty alleviation and employment programmes.
V	1993-	The panchayati raj renaissance phase: Constitutional status accorded to panchayats. Emphasis on preparation of area plans at all levels for economic development and social justice.

It may be seen that before 1993 the Indian Constitution did not specifically recognise the district as a third stratum of planning. Notwithstanding this constitutional lacuna, there have been some substantial experiences and achievements in decentralised planning in some states in the country during this phase (1951-93). Maharashtra and Gujarat in the western part of India have been the forerunners in this respect.[19]

Maharashtra innovated in the 1960s by devising a formula based on some managerial criteria for making district allocations from the state's 'divisible pool' which was pegged at 40 per cent of the total development funds of the state. Gujarat refined this procedure in the 1970s by providing for a modicum of 'un-tied funds' (along with an incentive grant) placed at the sole discretion of the local bodies for meeting their perceived needs. In both these states, elected local self-government institutions (PRIs) existed and were performing 'agency functions' for implementing specific development activities, devolved on them by the state government. But planning was deliberately kept out of their jurisdiction, and placed with institutional structures called 'District Planning and Development Councils', under a Minister of State as chairman. Initially, experiments in Maharashtra and Gujarat were hailed as a great success. But after sometime, contrary pulls affected the process of decentralisation. These consisted of diversion of funds assigned to the districts on the one hand, on the other, the growing reluctance and uneasiness among the elected state MLAs and MPs, and even the state cabinet, in parting with power and authority to the lower level-local bodies. With the passage of time, therefore, the role and the authority of the panchayats receded into the background, and that of the bureaucracy-backed by the Ministers, MLAs, and MPs-increased. Although some procedures followed for district planning in these states were innovative in character, they were more in the nature of a 'district budgeting' rather than a 'district planning' exercise (Sundaram 1979). In all these experiments, the façade of planning was sought to be kept, but the substance was lacking.[20]

As we proceed towards 1980s, some experiments were made to promote democratic institutions by securing greater participation by the people in local and governmental affairs in a few states like Karnataka and West Bengal. The large participatory character and involvement by local bodies and local people in planning and development was a distinctive departure in these exercises (Aziz *et al.* 1996; Lieten 1996; Meenakshisundaram 1994; Sundaram 1997).

But for these few isolated experiments, even now, the task of preparing a reasonably sound district plan has not made much headway in many other states. There are several reasons why it has not been possible (Sundaram 1997). Some of these are:

- Some lurking reluctance on the part of governments and their sectoral heads to devolve sufficient authority-administrative and financial-to the planning bodies at the district level.

- Lack of effective co-ordination at the district level between various agencies involved in the planning exercise.
- Institutionalised arrangements for seeking consultation with various participants in the planning process, were either not well established or nor sufficiently encouraged and developed.
- Lack of trained staff, both in terms of numbers as well as quality. The inadequacy of training is a serious constraint.[21]
- Lack of appropriate and reduced methodologies for planning, in tandem with the available capabilities at the local level.
- Planning without a clear and full understanding of the realities of resource constraints.
- The database presents its own problems. Although a surfeit of data is available at the local level from numerous sources, yet, appropriate methodologies have not emerged for selecting the 'critical minimum information' required for local planning and using the same for some simple analyses as a decision-support system.
- Lack of people's participation in planning was a serious constraint. There were no institutionalised 'pressure and user groups', that is 'poly-centric institutions' with the result that the local planning exercise was always at the mercy of people, who were not really interested in it (Sundaram 1997).

To sum up, the steps taken by different states during 1959 and 1993 to devolve powers and functions on Panchayati Raj bodies and to institute a systematic planning process were isolated, half-hearted and lacked clear direction. It is in the context of the above-mentioned weaknesses that a lot of determined efforts have now to be made for reorienting local planning structures and methodologies.

The Post-1993 Phase: Towards Decentralisation in a Multilevel Federalism

The new status accorded to the PRIs by the constitutional amendments has raised high hopes and expectations among the elected representatives and the rural folk at large. All the State Governments have enacted conformity state legislations, incorporating the provisions mentioned in the constitutional amendments and also held elections, in compliance with the centre's directives. With more than five years of working experience, the PRIs are going through 'a stage of transition and learning through experience'. With different political complexions of the governments in the Indian states, the passive attitude of the state-level political and administrative functionaries to part with power and authority, and some genuine financial and economic difficulties, the progress in operationalising decentralisation reforms has been somewhat slow and halting. The progress is also uneven among the states, partly owing to the lack of conceptual clarity in the constitutional amendment itself, which had left some vital discretionary powers with the states. Critics have pointed out that the gains have been in terms of 'democratic' improvements in the organisation of local-level panchayats which, however, are not commensurate with a clearly mandated functional agenda that will enable them to function as units of self-government.[22]

On the whole, the available evidence points to achievements that are 'nominal' or 'sub-nominal'. A recent evaluation by the National Institute of Rural Development says that 'while some of the states have regarded the systems essentially as an organisational set-up, emanating from the concept of democratic decentralisation, others have treated them merely as "agencies" for the implementation of rural development programmes. This approach eclipses the character of local bodies as "Units of self-government" (Choudhury and Jain 1999). It cannot be denied that in a complex issue like decentralisation reforms, with its multifarious components, the translation of vision into reality is a strenuous and slippery exercise. In fact, persistent efforts and constant persuasion are needed to materialize this. For instance, it has been argued that the newly elected representatives from the low-level strata of society, who are mostly illiterate, largely unaware of the political and economic dimensions of development issues in their areas, and lacking in planning and managerial skills, currently function as mere 'shadow politicians', virtually directed and controlled by the erstwhile political keymen of those areas, hailing from the rich and middle strata of the society. This is particularly true of elected women representatives who are performing under constraints of different kinds.[23]

A review of studies on panchayati performance conducted by various researchers (Aziz 1996; Mahipal 1998; Mishra *et al.* 1996; Pai 1998; Palanithurai 1997; Prashant *et al.* 1996; Singh 1985) shows that the elected members of Panchayati Raj Institutions were woefully lacking in their knowledge about their roles and responsibilities, particularly in regard to matters relating to planning.

Similarly, some field studies conducted in a state with which this author was associated, revealed that the elected sarpanchs totally lacked understanding about their roles and responsibilities, and had no skills in conducting the meetings of gram sabhas, with the result that they were never held. Even when held, gram sabha meetings were poorly attended. What was more distressing was that without any meaningful discussions really taking place, the minutes of the proceedings were written and signatures obtained by the village secretary, going from door to door. The lack of attendance of women in the meetings and the lack of participation by the poor and the Scheduled Castes were particularly striking. In another state (Madhya Pradesh), a dalit woman who had been elected as the President of the panchayats was not allowed to hoist the national flag on Republic Day, a privilege that naturally accrues to her as the elected chief of the area. In this state, many other atrocities were also committed on elected woman representatives, which have been documented (Mathew and Nayak 1996).[24]

The Key Issues

Such drawbacks have corrupted democracy in polarized societies in all corners of the world. Some seek to dismiss these as 'teething and transition problems', which may be solved in the course of time. Anyhow, the success of India's bottom democracies, which have to combine a certain amount of self-rule with shared rule in its federal principles, would depend upon how some of the key issues in local self-government are dealt with. These issues include:

- The effectiveness of local autonomy through devolution of functions and powers, keeping in view the principle of subsidiarity.
- The empowerment of the poor and the disadvantaged. The

effective capacitation of all actors involved in the democratic decentralisation process.[25]

- The manner in which the decentralised planning process is operationalised by the Panchayati Raj bodies, with the active assistance of technical experts, Community-Based Organizations (CBOs), other voluntary agencies, the bureaucratic machinery and the political authorities in the higher echelons of governments. The tasks involved here are colossal.

Challenges and Perspectives

In the first place, operationalising a multilevel planning process is a difficult task. It is a significant departure in the style, stance and substance of planning. 'Style' refers to the democratic and participatory character of planning; 'stance' refers to the 'people doing and government supporting a "two-way planning process"; and 'substance' refers to the programme and project components informed by the goals of growth, equity, stability and sustainability. In the new context, such planning is a democratic and technical exercise as well as management and negotiation process, to obtain the maximum benefits of development to the local population. For the local tiers of administration, who have so far been used to the centralised planning system-with its sectoral earmarking of funds and the mechanical implementation of the central/state sponsored schemes, hedged in by central/state guidelines-it is a new activity and poses a formidable challenge.[26]

Previously, no 'area plans' in the strict sense of the term, were prepared at all the three tiers of local administration. Of course, at the district level, plans were prepared by district administrations; but these were mainly in the form of assembling plans and schemes of various sectoral departments. Preparation of town plans were handled separately by urban development departments. However, there was no mechanism for integrating even these limited plans for rural and urban areas into a comprehensive district plan (Sundaram 1997). So far as the state plans were concerned, since their main constituents were the sectoral plans, it was only a matter of integrating them into the financial parameter, determined after discussions with the Central

Planning Commission. Now, with the Panchayati Raj system coming in the area plans prepared by the panchayats and consolidated by the district planning committees have to be assimiliated and harmonized into the state plan. Each state now has to devise its own mechanism and procedures for performing all these tasks.

Apart from the structural-functional aspects of planning, the states have also to meet the challenge of capacitation of the key personnel-both elected representatives and officials entrusted with the various tasks in planning. Assuming new responsibilities and becoming receptive to new ideas and behavioural patterns is not something that just 'falls from heaven'; instead, it has to be assiduously cultivated in a planned and purposeful manner. When all is said and done, the movement from 'centralism to decentralisation' at the local levels is a movement from 'dependency to discreet autonomy' in planning and development. It calls for the establishment of several 'prerequisites'. These include defining the functional, financial and administrative decentralisation procedures; establishing a time-bound planning process as well as procedures for integration; administrative arrangements for budgetary control, review, monitoring and evaluation of plans; and arrangements for the training of both officials and non-officials.[27]

The above preconditions demand both institutional and administrative changes. The states are still struggling to establish these prerequisites.

People's Participation

The most difficult aspect of the methodology here is ensuring the people's participation. The people here not only mean the elected bodies and officials, but also experts (academics), volunteers and the mass of people. In a success story, in a village called Kundrakudi in Tamil Nadu, which was documented by the Planning Commission in 1985, it was concluded that successful development requires a certain combination or 'mix' called, 'Technocratic, Academic and Democratic Mix' (TAD mix). To bring about this appropriate mix, a 'human catalyst' or 'social animator' is needed to see that things really work. In the case of Kundrakudi, it was a dedicated religious leader who was the, moving spirit' behind the transformation (Sundaram 1997). This is also confirmed from other similar success stories. In the Comilla model of rural development in Bangladesh, it was Akther Hameed Khan, a highly dedicated administrator turned social worker, who played the role of a catalyst. In Tachai in China, where the highest possible yields were obtained with hard work and a scientific approach to farming, it was Mao's clarion call for 'Learning from Tachai' that moved the masses. The dedication of the late President Park Chung Lee was responsible for the success of the Saemaul Undong movement in South Korea. Sukhomajri in Haryana state (India) owes its success story to the dedicated scientist P.R. Mishra. Instances of this kind can be multiplied to demonstrate the potency of the 'human factor' in development.[28]

In the area of decentralised planning, the Kerala example of 'People's Campaign' is a solitary case of a 'social movement approach', in which three million people (10 per cent of the total population of the state) took part in gram sabha meetings, that articulated local problems effectively and paved the way towards objective and community-specific local-level planning. All these examples show that in a highly fragmented society like ours, there is a need for some social trigger or catalyst, who can bring about a truly voluntary and conscious submerging of individual interests for the collective good of all. A thinker like Rajni Kothari has characterized this phenomenon of voluntarism and self-activity in our civilisational ethos, by the term 'the non-party political process' (Kothari 1998). Dantwala considers that voluntary action is both 'a combative and constructive force', or 'building a potent instrument for bringing about social transformation and an egalitarian and human society' (Dantwala 1998). However, replicating success stories and finding voluntary agencies with commitment to pro-poor values and working with dedication at the grass root level are difficult problems for any country.[29]

Translating the vision of democratic decentralisation into action in India is not just a problem of introducing new concepts. There are serious limitations in subverting the persistent caste system, feudal values, gender inequality, inhuman poverty conditions and the wide chasm existing between the rich and the deprived (Mathew 1997). Women, particularly those anchored in more 'traditional' conceptions and practices are slow to change. Social transformation is a difficult process of growing as individuals and collectivities. The process of change has to be consciously and consistently addressed in a continuous 'transitional development strategy', in which education, social uplift and change of the old order have to be important components. Obviously, this has to be an evolutionary process.

An Assessment and a Perspective

Planning, in India, has come a long way since its commencement in 1951. Starting primarily as a central activity, decentralisation at the first level, that is, the state, was accomplished in 1969 during the Fourth Plan period. The second stage of decentralisation at the local level, with constitutional backup, commenced after 1993. The governance and planning initiatives at the state level, over the years, have firmly established the democratic process and have also led to the laying down of some standard procedures for planning as well as the acquisition of some technical expertise for project formulation and monitoring and evaluation of plans. At the level of local bodies (PRIs), however, both decentralised governance and decentralised planning are facing conceptual as well as operational problems. The structures for local planning, that is, the shells, have been created; but without the kernel, they remain hollow. Obviously, the addition of a third stratum of PRIs had added enormous complexity to the Indian federal system, which has yet to be managed to satisfactory levels both structurally and politically.[30]

In an appraisal of the achievements so far, we may note that enfranchisement, empowerment and ethical functioning with a moral code of conduct, are the three elements of democratic decentralisation (Sundaram 1998). If democratic decentralisation is viewed as a 'stages approach' in transformation, it can be safely asserted that India has successfully crossed the first two stages (enfranchisement) and, has partially moved towards the 2nd stage (empowerment) with limited success. But what has been called the 'third wave of democratic transformation' (Dahl 1989), which is the 'ethical mode of functioning' is yet to be addressed in its totality. This is a process of consolidating democratic institutions, materializing the multilevel planning process and ensuring their effective functioning with some work ethics and managerial efficiency.

Acknowledgements: This is a modified and abridged version of three lectures, titled '*Planning Revisited: Rural Development in India-Vision and Reality*' delivered by the author on 15-16 November 1999 at Allahabad. The lectures were sponsored by the R.N. Dubey Memorial Foundation, Allahabad.

REFERENCES

Aziz, Abdul, Charles Nelson and Devendra Babu, 1996. "Power to the people". The Karnataka Experiment' in Abdul Aziz and David Arnold (ed.), *Decentralised Governance in Asian Countries*, pp. 146-63 New Delhi/Thousand Oaks/London: Sage Publications.

Aziz Abdul and P.V. Shenoy, 1997. 'District Planning, Principles and their operationalisation', *Journal of Rural Development*, 16(4).

Berry, B.J.L., 1996. "Essays on Commodity Flows and the Spatial Structure of the Indian Economy', *Research Paper III, University of Chicago*, Department of Geography.

Chakravarty, S., 1969. 'The Planning Process in India: An Appraisal and a Framework. New Delhi *Planning Commission* (mimeo).

Chidambaram, P., 1999. 'On *Spending Wisely*', L.K. Jha Memorial Lecture, Bharatiya Vidya Bhavan. (mimeo)

Choudhary, R.C. and S.P. Jain (eds.), 1999, Patterns of Decentralised Governance in Rural India, Vol. 1. Hyderabad: *National Institute of Rural Development*.

Dahl, Robert A., 1989. *Democracy and its Critics*, New Haven: Yale.

Dantwala, M.I., 1998. 'Promises to keep', in M.L. Dantwala, Harsh Sethi and Pravin Visaria (eds.). Social Change through Voluntary Action. New Delhi/Thousand Oaks/London: Sage Publications.

Gandhi, M.K., 1947, *Harijan*, 21 December.

GOI (Government of India, Planning Commission on Plan Projects), 1957. Report of the Study Team for the Study of National Extension Services, (Chairman, Balwantrai Mehta) Vol. 1, New Delhi 1969-74. '*Fourth Five Year Plan*', GOI.

Kothari, Rajni, 1998. 'The Future of Voluntarism', in M.L. Dantwala, Harsh Sethi and Pravin Visaria (eds.), *Social Change through Voluntary Action*. Chapter 12, New Delhi: Sage Publications.

Learmonth, A.T.A. and L.S. Bhat (eds.), 1962. Mysore State, Vol. 1: An Atlas of Resources (1960) and Calcutta : ISI.

and Mysore State, Vol. II: A Regional Synthesis (1962). Calcutta: ISI.

Lieten, G.K., 1996. *Development, Devolution and Democracy: Village Discourses in West Bengal*. New Delhi: Sage Publications.

Mahipal, 1998. "Women in Panchayats: Experience of a Training Camp', *Economic and Political Weekly*, January 24.

Mathew, George and Ramesh C. Nayak, 1996. 'Panchayats at Work: What it means for the Oppressed' *Economic and Political Weekly*, July 6.

Mathew, George, 1997. 'Panchayati Raj Structure and its Linkage to Development', in Pradeep Chaturvedi (ed.) *Food Security and Panchayati Raj*. New Delhi: Concept Publishing Co. Pvt. Ltd. New Delhi.

Mathur, Ashok, 1978. '*Regional Growth and Income Disparities in India*', New Delhi: Centre for Studies in Regional Development, Jawaharlal Nehru University (mimeo).

Mathur, P.C., 1995. 'The Constitutional Panchayats of India: Some Emerging Jurico-Philosophical Issues', in S.P. Jain and Thomas W. Hockgesang (eds.), Emerging Trends in Panchayati Raj (Rural Local Self-government) in India, pp. 5-21. Hyderabad: *National Institute of Rural Development and Konrad Adenauer Foundation.*

Meenakshisundaram, S.S., 1994. *Decentralisation in Developing Countries*. New Delhi Concept Publishing Co. Pvt. Ltd. New Delhi.

Mishra S.N. *et al.,* 1996. New Panchayati Raj in Action. New Delhi. Mittal Publications.

Misra R.P., K.V. Sundaram and V.L.S. Prakasa Rao, 1974. *Regional Development Planning in India*. A New Strategy. New Delhi: Vikas Publishing.

Mitra, Ashok, 1961. 'Levels of Regional Development in India', Census of India. Vol. 1 Part 1A(1). New Delhi: Government of India.

Moni, M., 1999. 'The Special Dynamics of Levels of Development in India',- A District level Analysis', New Delhi: *National Informatics Centre (mimeo).*

Nath, V., 1965. *Resource Development Regions and Divisions of India*. New Delhi: Planning Commission.

Pai, Sudha, 1998. 'Pradhans in the New Panchayats-Field Notes from Meerut', *Economic and Political Weekly*, 33(18).

Palanithurai, G., 1997. 'Capacity Building Exercise for Elected Representatives in Tamil Nadu', *Journal of Rural Development*, 16(4).

Prakasa Rao V.L.S., and L.S. Bhat, 1964. '*A Regional Framework for Resource Development', Geographical Magazine*, 19(1).

Prakasa Rao, V.L.S., K.V. Sundaram, R. Ramachandran and V.K. Tiwari, 1971. '*Regional Disparities in India*', Paper to the colloquium on Regional Inequalities of Development, I.G.U. Commission meetings, Rio-De-Janeiro, April.

Prashant *et. al.*, 1996. Popular Participation in Rural Development: Emerging Dynamics of Panchayati Raj Institutes in Haryana. Gurgaon: *Haryana Institute of Public Administration.*

Schwartzberg, J.E., 1962. 'Three Approaches to Mapping Economic Development in India', *Annals of the Association of American Geography*, 52.

Seers, Dudley, 1969. 'The Meaning of Development', *International Development Review* No. 4.

——1977. 'The New Meaning of Development', International Development Review, No. 3.

Sen Gupta, P. and Galina Sadasyuk, 1961, '*Economic Regionalisation of India-Problems and Approaches*', Census of India 1(8).

Singh, Hargian, 1985. *Panchayati Raj Administration in Haryana*. Gurgaon. Indira Publications.

Sundaram K.V., 1979. 'District Planning: The Case of Maharashtra', *Indian Journal of Public Administration*, No. 1 (January-March).

——1982. Geography of Underdevelopment: *The Spatial Dynamics of Underdevelopment*. New Delhi: Concept Publishing Co. Pvt. Ltd.

——1991. '*Decentralisation of Agricultural Planning for Ghana*', Rome: FAO (mimeo).

——1997. *Decentralized Multilevel Planning. Principles and Practice: Asian and African Experiences*. New Delhi Concept Publishing Co. Pvt. Ltd.

——1998. 'Transparency of the Planning Process and the Accountability of the Planning Institutions to the Local People'. Paper presented to the *World Bank sponsored National Workshop on Decentralised Rural Development*, 16-17 June.

——1999. 'Decentralised Planning and Financing of Rural Development in India' in *Regional Development Dialogue*, 20(2)

Sundaram, K.V. and V.L.S. Prakasa Rao, 1971. 'Regional Planning in India', Paper presented at the *21st International Geographical Congress Symposium on Regional Planning* (published by the National Committee for Geography, Calcutta).

Vyas, V.S., Anil Bhatt and S.M. Shah, 1985. *Decentralised Planning in India*. New Delhi: Oxford University Press and IBH Publishing Co.

18

Prof. S.P. Chatterjee, as I know him

When I was requested to speak a few words about Prof. S.P Chatterji the father of Indian Geography, I was too happy. I decided to summon up from my storehouse of memories, of a person, whom I greatly revered and respected. I decided to summon up from my storehouse of memories, some remembrances of things past about him. They are sweet remembrances and my highly cherished ones.

I had the good fortune of personally knowing Prof. Chatterjee, if I recall from the year 1962. It was Prof. Prakasa Rao who introduced me to him. Since then, I used to meet him more often whenever he was in Delhi. Sometimes, I used to discuss my research work with him. It was the 1968 IGU Congress that brought me closer to him. At that time, all his energies were bent in organizing the Congress meticulously. As you all know, the Congress was a great success. Prof. Chatterjee asked me and Prof. Prakasa Rao to give as much help as possible to the Congress Secretariat, which was manned by Prof. T.R. Lakshmanan's wife. We used to spend some evenings chalking out various Technical Sessions.

While drawing up the programme for the plenary sessions for the Congress, Prof. Chatterjee told Shri C.S. Chandrasekara, a well known Town Planner and myself to prepare for holding a special session on "Planning Regions of India" and place the TCPO's scheme of Inter-State Regions of India for discussion before a larger audience. Accordingly, this was discussed in a special session with eminent

---

Lecture Delivered on the birth centenary Celebration of Prof. S.P. Chatterjee, November 2002 at New Delhi.

geographers like Prof. Brian Berry, Prof. Schwartzberg, Prof. Learmonth and many others including some Russian Geographers being present. Later, in one of his meetings with Prof. Gadgil, Dy. Chairman of the Planning Commission, Prof. Chatterjee along with Prof. Prakasa Rao commended the notion of constituting Inter-State Economic Regions for the formulation of Regional Policies. This was a new idea at that time, viz. introducing a new geographical scale in planning when the State Governments were not adequately equipped technically to man their own planning departments. This led to the project on "The Regional Development Plan for the South-East Resource Region", with which I was associated during those days. Despite our hard work—I called it in one of my papers as a "Work of some awesome earnestness"—it ended as an abortive effort due to various political happenings. Anyhow I don't go into those issues.

In my own personal life and career, Prof. Chatterjee was a great source of encouragement and inspiration. I recall an incident. It was in the Population Geography Symposium of the IGU. I had prepared a paper titled "The Town Group: An Operational Concept", in which I had drawn the distinction between the "Political or Administrative City" and the "Geographical City" and pleaded for the delimitation of 'Standard Urban Areas' for Census Operations. The Government of India accepted the idea and myself from the TCPO and Dr. Roy Burman from The Census office jointly worked on this project. When Prof. Chatterjee came to know about it, he wrote a very nice letter to me encouraging me to continue with innovative ideas and projects. In the Preface to the Proceedings of the Symposium on Population Geography, published by the National Committee for Geography, Calcutta in 1971, he wrote:

"One of the most important recommendations arising from discussions which followed K.V. Sundaram's paper was that Geographical Aspects should be taken into account in delimiting urban tracts and the concept of "Town Group" adopted by the Census Organization in India should be reconsidered in the light of this problem. We are happy to note that in pursuance of this recommendation, it has since been decided to delimit the urban tracts on the basis of the concept of the "Standard Urban Areas".

I quote this as an indication of the generous nature in Prof.

Chatterjee, the human being, who always tried to encourage and support every contribution that was good. It also shows that he was immune from that most common vile of human faults-jealousy. I heard him saying that "God has given everyone some talents and we should help him use it to the benefit of others".

He had an intellectual and moral courage of a special kind. He could be obstinate and strict as a research guide, as Prakasa Rao used to tell me. But at the same time, this was not a vice. It was a courage of his conviction that Doctoral Students must earn their degrees from hard field work and empiricism. In his view, their work should become their lifetime specialization and must be recognized as such. He scoffed at those Universities, who were lowering their standards and awarding degrees for mediocre students. Prof. Chatterjee's students are spread in different parts of the country and they bear witness to his great qualities of the head and the heart.

He was a great visionary and a man of great achievements. I recall the Book that he brought out—50 years of Indian Geography—at the time of the 1968 Congress. Many of his students toiled hard at it and brought it out at the nick of time. It is important to note that this work initiated by him was the prelude to the series of publications brought out by the ICSSR later on under the title "Survey of Research in Geography". Prof. Chatterjee was the pioneer in this regard.

Prof. Chatterjee was a great crusader of noble causes. He was the most modern and progressive thinker of his times and a dynamic leader in Geography. His leadership qualities were impeccable. Immediately after the International Conference, he lobbied for two things to lift the image of Geography—one for a National Atlas Organization and another for a National Institute for Geography. As it was told to me, the Prime Minister asked him to name one project which he considered as priority and he named the National Atlas Project. Thus it was that his dream for the establishment of the National Atlas and Thematic Mapping Organization (NATMO) was realised. We have with us here his second successor, Dr. Prithvish Nag, who has carried forward Prof. Chatterjee's dreams to the highest pitch. You all know the reputation that NATMO enjoys in the country and abroad with its excellent contributions. You have also seen the recognition accorded to Dr. Nag in appreciation of his services. We congratulate him on his appointment as Surveyor General of India and for being the foremost torchbearer of Prof. Chatterjee's tradition of dedicated and hard work to achieve great things.

Lastly, I must say that besides NATMO, Prof. Chatterjee struggled and strived during his lifetime to make Geography an acceptable discipline in the Universities and paved the way to create and establish new Departments of Geography in the country. His path was uphill all the way. In the later years of his life, in spite of his failing health, he used to go and lecture in many places to promote the cause of Geography.

Prof. Chatterjee also developed spiritual inclinations and became a devotee of Shri Satya Sai Baba. He did some notable work on the Geography of Culture and Religion too. He did an in-depth Geographical Analysis on the route taken by Shri Rama and Seetha to Sri Lanka and delivered popular lectures on this theme. Shri Satya Sai Baba invited him to the Whitefield in Bangalore to deliver this lecture in his Institution. During this lecture, he became suddenly ill and Baba revived him. On that day, I was in Mysore to deliver a lecture in a Training Programme. Later, Prof. Misra and myself, listened to Prof. Chatterjee narrating his marvellous spiritual experience. He remained an ardent devotee of Shri Satya Sai Baba.

I feel proud that I have had the pleasure of personally knowing and interacting with this legendary figure in our profession, a doyen of Geography, a matchless and multi-faceted personality and a person who was instrumental in lifting the image of Geography and placing it as one among the respectable disciplines in Social Sciences.

Friends, I pay my humble homage to the departed soul of this great person, who is watching the developments in Geography from the Heavens. Let us be worthy of him and assure him that we are following his sacred path.

Index